THE
POSTER
BOY

THE
POSTER
BOY

SMALL TOWNS, BIG IDEAS, AND THE REALITY OF BECOMING AN ENTREPRENEUR

CHAD SCOTT

I first met Chad Scott while he was waiting tables at a J Alexanders outside Chicago. The friend I was with just happened to mention this "really cool guy" with a "really cool business" that he was starting. I thought to myself, 'O Lord, here we go.' But as soon as I met Chad, I knew he was nothing like all the other entrepreneurs who've come to knock at my door. And the business he was beginning to build was nothing like the umpteen other boring ideas I've had pitched to me over the years.

Chad was ready to go... literally. In the middle of his shift, he folded up his apron and led me out to his car. He popped the trunk and walked me through the inventory of products he was developing. They were all great, but what interested me most was Chad himself. He had a glow about him, like he was ready to conquer the world. He didn't drink, smoke, or do drugs; the infectious energy Chad gave off was 100% natural, and there was no way he was about to let anything blunt his edge. Impressed, I asked him what in the world he was doing waiting tables. When he told me he needed to clear some debt before he could get his business off the ground, I couldn't help myself. I pulled a check from my wallet, wrote it out for $4,000, and told him to get to work.

Don't look at me; that "early investment" was all about *Chad* and what I saw in *him*. He reminded me of myself when I was younger. He had it in him to make his own mark—to do the right thing, learn from every mistake, and strive to improve himself, his business, and the world. I've met very few people like Chad—I was honored to be featured alongside many of them in Rhonda Byrne's book *The Secret*—and they've all shared that same undeniable spark. World-conquerors like Chad will inspire and motivate you without even trying. They're incredibly rare. So, whenever I meet one, I stop what I'm doing and I pay attention. If you want to succeed in business *and* life, that's what exactly what you'll do with Chad's book: pay attention.

I'm impressed by what Chad's accomplished, but I'm not surprised. I could see what Chad would accomplish long before it ever came to pass. By having conversations with him over the years and becoming close friends, it was obvious that Chad would be successful in every sense of the word. More than 30 locations across the U.S., over 130 team members in multiple offices around the globe, millions of dollars in annual revenue— these are just a few of the "standard" marks of success in business. But Chad is anything but standard. Just ask the people who go to work for him every day.

Chad hasn't just created a company; he's created a *team* where people genuinely care for one another and never stop playing to win. It's one thing to get people to work for you; it's something else to keep them excited and engaged on the job. I've never seen anything quite like the way Chad inspires before he hires (and after). Especially with the millennial and Gen Z kids who so many of the leaders in my generation have given up on, Chad has shown time and again and that he isn't giving up on *anyone*. I've watched him go into high schools and inspire teenagers to dream bigger than they ever thought, and to join him in building something better than they ever could've dreamed.

You might think a guy like Chad would think he's got the world figured out. Not so. Two things have impressed me about Chad from day one: his humility in reaching out for help and his gratitude for sound advice. When you talk to Chad, he listens. He engages and asks good questions. He receives constructive criticism. He actually *takes* the advice your offer and puts it to work—like the time when I said he should outsource his graphic design and he turned that simple advice into huge value for both his business *and* two whole communities in Mexico. Chad takes advice better than anyone I know. I can assure you, that's a huge part of why he is where he is today.

So, now it's your turn for some advice. Back when I first met Chad, I told him you have to be incredibly careful who you listen to. If someone tells you how to be happy, you better find out whether they're truly happy. If someone wants to show you how to make money, you better take a look at their bank statement before you buy whatever they're selling. And if someone wants to teach you how to succeed in life and business, you better make sure they've walked the walk before you spend a couple hundred pages "listening" to them talk. I'm happy to say that Chad has done just that. Take my advice and listen to what he has to say.

Life makes it too easy to accept the limitations of your current circumstances, especially if you're still living under your parents' roof. As

Chad says again and again in the book, we become who we're around. If you don't look outside your social and family circles for motivation and guidance, you'll never get beyond what they've accomplished in life. If you don't put yourself into circumstances that stretch you, you'll never grow. This book is a story about a guy who's done exactly that and experienced phenomenal success as a result. Better for you, it's a helpful guide to how you can do the same. Chad came from nowhere and started with nothing, yet he managed to solve one problem after another until he could get his business off the ground. You may not be Chad, but that doesn't matter. The problem-solving and business-building skills he shares here are clear, accessible, and thoughtfully packaged to help you move forward, even if you're nowhere and you're starting with nothing.

The world is just now getting to see what I've had the privilege of seeing for years. Chad makes everyone around him better—including me. I know that after you've spent some time with him in this book, you'll be better too. Just turn the page and you'll see.

PETER FOYO
CEO, Principal Standard Group
Former CEO & Chairman, Nextel de Mexico

CONTENTS

CHAPTER 01

Beach Blankets and Legal Battles

> **"**ALL OUR DREAMS CAN COME TRUE, IF WE HAVE THE COURAGE TO PURSUE THEM.
>
> WALT DISNEY

A little over 15 years ago, one of my favorite college professors taught me a lesson I'll never forget: you can tell a lot about a business by the quality of its problems. From one angle, you could describe my entire entrepreneurial career as an exercise in learning just what those words mean. From the early days of designing posters in a college dorm and selling them to youth sports teams down to today—managing a global business with 31 locations across the U.S., 2 offices in Mexico, 1 in Indonesia, and more than 130 team members—the problems I've faced have said more about my business than any profit and loss statement ever could.

As true as my professor's words are for business (we'll unpack this idea later on), they're even more true for life in general. The quality of your life will depend on the problems you face and the solutions you find. Will you run and hide, or will you face up to them, ask hard questions, and work to move forward? Will today's problems become tomorrow's proverbs about life and success, or will they just turn into another heap of excuses for never becoming who you know you were supposed to become? No matter what problems I've run into—as you'll see, I've had to face some ridiculous stuff—the through-line of my life has been a relentless commitment to growth and innovation.

This book is my story. More than that, it's a testimony to what can happen when you grab hold of an idea, grit your teeth, and take a blind leap into the darkness, trusting you'll find your way to the other side. Don't get me wrong; this isn't a puff piece. I've built something I can be proud of, but I don't think I've "arrived." In the following pages, I hope you'll join me as I narrate my crazy journey as an entrepreneur. Along the way, I'll give you all the practical advice I wish I had so that you can avoid my mistakes and save yourself all the detours I had to take. But before we can get where we're going, I need to tell you a few things about where we are today.

Trouble Out of Paradise

In one form or another, I've spent the past 15 years building my company, Ultimate Team Products (UTP), from the ground up. Recently, one of my closest partners and I decided we needed to take a moment to step away from the business and let it run without us in the day-to-day picture. So, I rounded up my wife (Mary) and our three kids (Brady, Jordan, and Addison), my partner grabbed her boyfriend, and the 7 of us went off to spend an entire month in Cancun.

This was the first time we felt we'd built something that could survive without us, so we took the risk and left. That trip turned out to be exactly what *everybody* needed. UTP didn't just survive while we were gone. It thrived. That January, our sales spiked higher than they'd ever been. When I saw that, I felt I'd truly jumped the gap from self-employed to a business owner. With the help of some amazing people, I'd finally built a platform that could allow others to make a quality living, do something they enjoy, and generate a healthy profit—all without me having to stand there and look over everybody's shoulder.

So far, that sounds like the standard entrepreneur's life, right? Work a little, play a lot. Make a few calls, then disappear to the beach for weeks on end. Well, that may be the picture most people see when they think of entrepreneurs and startups, but the real world of business is much more gritty. And in case I was tempted to think I'd "arrived," a cold dose of reality was waiting for me when we arrived back home: a lawsuit.

Mo' Money, Mo' Problems?

It may not seem like it from our month in Cancun, but my family and I live small. We always have, and we always will. Even though UTP has grown more than I ever could've dreamed, we've intentionally chosen to take a modest paycheck from the company, live within our means, and stay as far away from debt as we possibly can. The Mexico trip was a long overdue vacation, and we were able to pull it off by utilizing many of the skills we've developed in building our business—resourcefulness, planning, and dogged attention to expenses. We booked our oceanfront condo through Airbnb *6 months in advance*. We researched public transit and realized we didn't need to rent a car. "Small" moves like these may seem like a hassle, but they're more than just a few tactics for saving money on a family vacation; they're the unavoidable habits that have made it possible for us to scale a business from peanuts to millions—all with very little outside capital.

Keeping with our vow to live small, my family lives in an average house in an inexpensive neighborhood. Instead of selling our souls to Wells Fargo for the privilege of life in the *cul de sac*, we wanted our lives to stay simple and mortgage-free. For the most part, we keep to ourselves. When people ask me what I do, I tell them I'm a graphic designer. Still, when they see the Tesla I drive, they assume I'm some kind of a rockstar. Far from it. The thing I love most about my car is how I paid for it. Out of little more than admiration for Tesla and its CEO (Elon Musk), I took my hard-earned profit and bought stock in the company. When that stock just so happened to skyrocket, I sold my shares and bought myself the only car I'd ever truly desired.

Whether you flaunt it or not, success is enough to draw the wrong kind of attention from people who'd like nothing more than to skim a little bit off your top. Here's a lesson I've learned and will share throughout this book: you are the sum of the people you spend the most time with and the books you read. Surround yourself with quality people and you'll become a quality person. Allow yourself to be surrounded by less than quality people, and you'll find it much more difficult to grow in a positive direction. Worst-case scenario, one or two of them will come after your livelihood.

That's exactly what happened when I came home from Cancun to find that lawsuit waiting in my mailbox. I'm not at liberty to discuss the details right now, but suffice it to say that the suit itself is utter nonsense. From what I've been able to gather so far, the "facts" of the suit don't even come close to lining up with reality. The only real motivation I can find has more to do with grabbing an easy payday from me personally than recouping some legitimate expense. Am I worried about it? Absolutely not. This is what happens when you start to succeed in life and business. In a way, this is the kind of problem I hope you'll have to deal with some day if you keep reading this book.

Not My First Legal Rodeo

Though not directly related to my business, the lawsuit I found waiting for me is just one of the many unique problems that have spurred me to grow as both an entrepreneur and a human being. I wish I could say this was my first "opportunity" to grow through litigation, but it wasn't. Back in 2017, UTP decided to experiment with something like a franchising model. I say "something like" because we were never able to dial in all the legalities—a minor "detail" that'd come to bite me later. Long story short, the model didn't work for us from a financial or branding standpoint. Customer service has always been a core value of mine, so to hand control off to "franchisees" always rubbed me the wrong way. They never seemed to take care of our partners and customers the way *I* would take care of them, so we ended up saying goodbye to that little misadventure.

Before we decided to nix the franchise model, we met a woman in Seattle through a tournament director I'd come to trust and appreciate. Let's call her Sally. She was eager—maybe, too eager—to take on a UTP franchise, so we hooked her up with the financing she'd need and squared away *most of* the legal paperwork. But, before the ink on our contract was even dry, Sally took a hard right turn. We thought we were getting a partner, but she quickly became an adversary. As far as Sally was concerned, we were out to take advantage of her, and she wasn't about to let that happen. We butted heads *constantly*. Anytime we tried to reign her in, she'd berate us and threaten to break off on her own. She had no idea what it took to build UTP but thought she could copy our entire business model with a handful of graphic designers and an HP DesignJet. She was obviously wrong, but I didn't take it as anything more than trash talk. I was wrong.

Business is about relationships. If you take care of people, they'll take care of you. If you treat people with dignity and respect, they'll return the favor. When you take the time to connect with your suppliers on a *human* level, you develop a bond that goes beyond dollars and cents. So, when a jilted franchisee tries to go behind your back and work a side deal without your knowledge, you can expect those very same suppliers to turn right around and let you know what's going on.

As soon as we found out Sally was trying to make good on her threats to steal our business, we decided enough was enough. We weren't just going to cut her loose, we were going to drag Sally into court and punch her right in the mouth—legally speaking, of course. We found a local lawyer to represent us. Our case was strong, but we needed to arbitrate the case in Washington. So, we pulled a few lawyers from Seattle onto the team. They were rock stars and we were ready to throw down. At least, we thought we were ready. Come to find out, we missed a few pieces of key paperwork in Washington. Sally's lawyers did what lawyers do and tore us to shreds in arbitration. Heading into that battle, we fully expected to win $25,000—just enough to recoup the money we'd lost on Sally. In retreat, we were grateful we only had to pay $50,000 in legal fees. Worse, we had to agree to keep UTP out of Seattle and Las Vegas until 2020. As exhausting as that entire process was, I consider it an investment in my growth. I'm not the same guy I was before we went to war with Sally. And you better believe I've learned some things about franchises, lawyers, and paperwork.

Why the Stories and Why the Book

Why should you care about where I've been, what I've built, who I've sued, and who's sued me? For one thing, I want you to know that "the entrepreneur's life" is anything but "Lifestyles of the Rich and Famous." Beyond that, I want to tell my story as a way of giving back to the people who've been alongside me and paying it forward to people who'll come behind me. An Irish philosopher named Edmund Burke once said, "Example is the school of mankind, and they will learn at no other." Like any successful entrepreneur, artist, or athlete will tell you, we learn our best lessons from watching others, especially when they fall flat on their faces. As I said at the beginning of this chapter, the problems I've faced have shaped me as a person. They've profoundly impacted the way I see and think about things. This book is my way of inviting readers into that story. My sincere hope is that you'll pick up a few valuable life and business lessons that'll help *you* build something you can be proud of.

More than a storybook full of motivation and inspiration, though, I wanted to write something practical. For the past 15 years, I've had to figure most of this stuff out on my own. I've had a few great mentors along the way, but I've always had to rely on the bits and scraps of practical advice I could pick up in business books. Even there, I never found a how-to guide. Setting up a business, cobbling together legal paperwork, building out manufacturing, nurturing a supply chain, developing partnerships—these are all things I had to figure out on my own. I had to create my own path. That's why, I didn't want to leave this book at just my story. I want readers like you to have a practical guide to actually *doing* this stuff. That's why every other chapter in this book will focus on concrete advice, giving you the practical steps you need to think through ideas, raise money, go to market, and do everything else it takes to build a successful business.

Is It All Worth It?

I spend a lot of time with high school students and young adults talking about life and business. The image so many of them have is that life as an entrepreneur is life on the beach (Cancun above). The reality, though, is more like wrangling with shiesty acquaintances and shady business partners. Most people, high school kids or otherwise, expect business to be all sunshine and roses. The minute things get hard, they either think they're doing it wrong or business just isn't for them. My argument is always this: they're *not* doing it wrong and it *is* for them. Business is supposed to be hard; anything worth doing is hard. The question is, how will you respond to the challenge?

Business is hard, but it's worth it. Going into business has shaped me as a person. It's allowed me to dodge the primary workforce, which is huge as far as I'm concerned. It's given me the chance to build something I'm passionate about and to gather a community of people who care about my vision as much as I do. The connections I've developed with team members, partners, tournament directors, and suppliers have been some of the deepest and most rewarding relationships I've ever known.

Money has never been the primary motivator for me. I've got nothing against people who want to start a business and make a ton of cash. The only question I'd ask is this: what do you think that money will get you? A big house? A fancy car? Confidence? Happiness? There's nothing wrong with any of those things, but here's the deal. Big houses come with even bigger mortgages. Even fancy cars rust over time. Confidence only comes from competence. Happiness isn't for sale. Make all the money you want, but don't ask it to do for you what only *you* can do for yourself. I don't care what your bank account says; you'll only ever be as successful as you *think* and *feel* you are.

As I've shared above, there's so much more to building a business than making buckets of money. If you want to be a part of what Tim Ferriss calls the "new rich," it's not about having $1 million in the bank. Instead, it's about having residual income and being able to generate that money from anywhere—whether you're in Rockdale, Illinois or Cancun, Mexico. Even if your business "only" generates $5,000-worth of monthly residual income, you've got enough to literally move *anywhere* and do *anything* you want. Flexibility and freedom to be who you want to be, do what you want to do, and pursue what you want to pursue—*that's* what entrepreneurship can do for you.

Conclusion

You can tell the quality of a person's life by the quality of their problems. For me, the last 15 years have been one massive adventure in problem-solving. With every new solution came a new set of challenges, and with every step forward came a new world of possibility for me to navigate. I've experienced incredible highs. I've suffered through debilitating lows. It's been a fantastic story, but I'll be the first to admit that I'm still in the middle of it. I haven't "arrived," and I don't know how this story ends. But what I do know is this: other people's stories have the power to grab us by the scruff of our neck and launch us out into the world. I wouldn't tell you mine unless I was truly convinced you could learn from my losses and find motivation in my wins. Are you ready to see what a *real* entrepreneur's life looks like? Better, are you ready to learn what it takes to build a life you can live on your own terms? Then strap in. We're just getting started.

CHAPTER 02

When Things Get Hard

> " TOUGH TIMES NEVER LAST,
> BUT TOUGH PEOPLE DO.
>
> ROBERT H. SCHULLER

When you print posters for a living, you spend a lot of money on ink. In 2016, we had about 50 Canon printers we used at all our sites across the country. So, when a supplier from China offered to supply our ink for a tenth of what we had been paying, I was immediately interested. And when they told me they could put our branding on the box, I was pretty well sold. Of course, I needed to test the product first, so I ordered a small batch, set up a printer in the garage, and printed through an entire roll of paper. I liked what I saw. In fact, it was flawless. Next step: I ordered $30,000-worth of the stuff. Like I said, when you print posters for a living, you spend a lot of money on ink.

Soon enough, I managed to get the new ink out to all my crews in the field. Within the first few hours of putting it into our printers, I got the first call: "Hey, Chad, my printer isn't printing red or magenta." At first,

I wasn't that concerned. This kind of thing happens. So, I had my guy do a head clean. No dice. Then, the other phone calls started rolling in: "My cyan isn't working. My blacks aren't showing up." I turned green. I had a nationwide debacle on my hands. If I didn't figure something out quick, I'd lose an entire weekend-worth of revenue.

Right away, I called up Canon for help. I told them we were having issues with our print heads, and they asked me for our printer cartridge numbers. When I couldn't find the number, they had me send in a photo. As soon as the photo hit that support representative's screen, she knew we'd gone outside of Canon's ecosystem to purchase our ink. About a millisecond later, she voided the warranty on all 50 of our printers. Just like that, we lost $250,000 in ink and equipment—all because I was trying a little too hard to cut our expenses. It was a massive loss, and we were lucky to just barely stay alive through it. Let's call that one very expensive lesson learned.

Get Ready for Adversity

Legendary football coach Lou Holtz once said, "Show me someone who has done something worthwhile, and I'll show you someone who has overcome adversity." Especially for business owners, those words are spot on. You've never met a successful person in business who *hasn't* had to overcome his or her fair share of adversity. The story I shared above is just one striking example of the hurdles I've had to overcome in building UTP. But it's not the only example. In fact, it's not even one of the hardest ones.

Adversity in business is about more than just an expensive lapse in judgment or a deal gone bad. It doesn't always come with a price tag, and it's rarely ever straight-forward. Sometimes, adversity looks like the subtle gnaw of people you love and respect who don't believe in what you're trying to do. Other times, it looks (and feels) like a metaphorical knife in your back. I've known adversity from both those angles and more. I've had people I care about tell me to my face that I'd never amount to anything. I've had a good friend—someone I grew up with—work with me for years and then turn around and start his own competing business using contacts he got from me.

Stuff like this always hurts, and it can threaten to derail *any* entrepreneur. I don't care how tough you are; adversity cuts deep. If you're not ready for it, it'll tank your business before it even gets off the ground. One of the most important questions you can ask yourself in the beginning, then, is this: how will I prepare myself to meet adversity?

LEARN FROM OTHERS

The first, most important thing you can do to prepare for adversity is to read about what others have done to accomplish their dreams— especially those who've had to overcome long odds. Here are 6 books that have shown me what adversity looks like and have given me the tools and inspiration to charge ahead:

- *Shoe Dog,* **Phil Knight** - This book tells the story of Phil Knight, the founder of Nike. Knight started his business with a $50 loan from his father and a mission to import high-quality sneakers from Japan. In 1963, Knight grossed $8,000 selling his shoes out of the trunk of his car. Today, Nike's sales top $30 billion.
- *Made in America,* **Sam Walton** - Everyone knows Sam Walton as the founder of Walmart. Even though his store put my dad out of a job (see chapter 3), I can appreciate Walton's mission to turn a single dime-store into the largest retailer in the world.

- *Rich Dad, Poor Dad,* **Robert T. Kiyosaki** - This is the #1 Personal Finance book of all time. More importantly, it's a book about mindset. Kiyosaki teaches his readers that "getting rich" is about a lot more than luck and education. It takes work—smart work—that anyone can do.
- *Delivering Happiness,* **Tony Hsieh** - As the founder of Zappos, Tony Hsieh has established himself as the master of workplace culture. He's had to go through a lot in building his company. His story is powerful and motivational; it'll make you want to go out and create the best business you possibly can.
- *The Secret,* **Rhonda Byrne** - This book has motivated me in virtually every aspect of my life. We all have power deep within us. Byrne helps us tap into that power and use it to charge through adversity towards success.
- *The 4-Hour Workweek,* **Timothy Ferriss** - At a practical level, this book is solid gold. It isn't about cutting your work week down so much as it's about multiplying your productivity and efficiency tenfold. The advice in this book is crucial for anyone looking to start a business in our world today.

The value of books like these isn't *just* their stories of adversity and grit. More than giving you an inspiring anecdote to hold on to, they train your mind as an entrepreneur. They give you the depth and insight you need to anticipate key moments in the road ahead. By crawling into the heads of the authors I've listed above, you'll better prepare yourself for the journey ahead. You'll also give yourself the solid base of knowledge you need to plan (as much as possible) for the inevitable bumps ahead.

EXPECT REJECTION

Rejection is a normal part of business. Partners will tell you you're nothing special (they've done it to me!). Potential customers will say your product is lame. Some investors will hate your idea. Distributors will give you the brush-off. It's not a matter of *if* these things will happen but *when*. If you don't prepare yourself for the inevitable rejection you're going to face, you'll whither in the face of it. Learn to expect rejection and you'll thicken your skin enough to let it roll off your back. Factor it into your success as just another necessary step on the journey. If you know you've got a conversion rate of 10%, then go out and gladly endure the 9 no's you need to hear to finally get your yes. Treat them like reps at the gym. They hurt like crazy, but the product is worth the pain.

PLAN FOR EVERY POSSIBLE CONTINGENCY

At the beginning of my journey with UTP, I'd just make a decision and go with it, letting the chips fall wherever they fell. Today, I've learned to stop and play out every decision before jumping in with both feet. Drawing on my own experience and the wisdom of trusted advisors, I think several steps ahead of myself to see how my actions might play out in our business. That kind of anticipation is crucial in preparing for adversity. Taking the time to sit and think about potential outcomes for each and every decision will save you an incredible amount of time, money, and heartache.

PREPARE TO SCRAP YOUR PLAN

As smart as it is to anticipate the future and plan for contingencies, you're not a fortune-teller. You can't anticipate every bump in the road before it happens. Back in 2012, we were a leading consumer of frames from the popular hobby chain Michaels Stores. We had a good thing going with Michaels; they supplied our frames at a great price and we enjoyed a healthy margin. That all changed, though, when we started noticing a slip in quality. Our contingency plan was to find a new supplier, but we found out quickly that replacing Michaels was much easier said than done.

There's no amount of planning we could've done to anticipate the convoluted road we had to walk to figure out who would supply our frames and how. Hard up for another supplier that'd allow us to hold on to our healthy margins, we eventually decided to start a framing company in Texas with the help of one of my relatives. After 6 months of struggling to make that work, we gave up and settled on a supplier in Georgia. Problem solved, right? Yes, but only for a little while. Eventually, the supplier hiked their prices and, once again, we were stuck looking for someone else to make our frames.

OWN YOUR ADVERSITY

We knew we couldn't perpetuate the cycle of new frame suppliers and jacked-up prices, so we finally decided to bite the bullet and start our *own* framing operation in-house. I'll tell you more about that story later on in the book (trust me, you'll want to stick around for that). For now, though, it's important to point out that we never ran away from the problem. We didn't pretend as though Michaels' slip in quality wasn't a problem. We didn't settle for the status quo with our company in Texas or our supplier in Georgia. It would've been "easy" to let those things slide and focus elsewhere.

But the easy thing is rarely the right thing. And the way to overcome adversity isn't to pretend it isn't there but to embrace it and get to work on finding solutions. The problems you ignore *will* come back to bite you. Shoddy frames would've earned us a shabby reputation. Narrower margins would've compromised our ability to grow and expand into new markets. If we wanted to keep moving forward, we needed to acknowledge our problem, put our heads down, and *solve* it. So, we gamed out the problem from every angle we could, tapped all the resources we could find, scribbled our way through a stack of cocktail napkins, leaned on advisors for help, and improvised our way out of that mess and into a solution that served us well for years to come.

FAIL SMALL, FAIL OFTEN

What does it look like to own your adversity and march forward through the complicated mess of life in a startup? It looks like failure—lots of it. You have to come to grips with this immutable reality: you're going to fail time and again as you work your way to success. That just comes with the territory. Remember what Lou Holtz said about adversity? He could've just as easily said it about failure. There isn't a successful person in the world who hasn't failed over and over again on their way to the top. Henry Ford, Bill Gates, J.K. Rowling—those are just a few names of people who fell flat on their face before they could rise up to glory in their respective industries.

Failure is easy to swallow in the beginning. You've just gotten started, your budget is small, and there's nobody counting on you to deliver. If you're at the beginning of your entrepreneurial journey, take that reality and run with it. Let it be your license to improvise and take risks. Fail small; if something isn't working then don't be afraid to give it the ax before it turns into a colossal money trap. Fail often; the virtue of a lean startup is your ability to pivot on a dime. Without a massive organization to steer, you can change direction without having to create too many waves.

It's when you get into the middle range that failure becomes much more difficult to stomach. It's one thing to screw up when your business consists entirely of you, a dorm room, and a laptop. It's quite another when you've got around 130 team members to think about. At that point, you can't pivot on a dime. You've got to take your turns wide and slow, thinking 10 steps ahead of every decision to ensure you've got your bases covered in every possible dimension. At this level, the need to fail small and often becomes even more critical. If you want to make something happen, you need to test, refine, rinse, and repeat before you can even think about rolling out a change at the organizational level. Remember the ink fiasco? It turned out I didn't do *enough* small work in order to make sure the ink would work at the larger level. And I paid the price.

Dealing with Negativity

I'm going to let you in on something that's bugged me for almost 20 years: my high school classmates *didn't* vote me most likely to succeed in our senior yearbook. Of course, they did the right thing. Nobody in Kennett had any reason to believe I'd go anywhere. Still, that high school yearbook serves as just one token example of a trend I've seen along the way—an ugly reality every entrepreneur needs to come to grips with early on: others' negativity.

In building my business, I've met more naysayers than I can count—people who were secretly (and not-so-secretly) rooting for me to fail. Whenever you leave (whether it's a small town or the rat race), you can always count on grief from the people who've stayed behind. They see your decision to live a better, fuller life as a condemnation of their own. They take a look at your college experience, success in business, and wonderful family, then decide that you must think you're better than them. Of course, that's not the reality, but it's the perception. And whether they say it to your face or not, they would love nothing more than for the world to take you down a peg or two.

Of course, true friends and family will come along who *genuinely* want to see you win. Hold on to those people for dear life. They're the exception. What do you do with the rest, though? How do you handle the onslaught of negativity you're bound to experience once you start moving forward in business? My answer: develop a habit of generosity. Regardless of what you get from people, lavish positivity on others. Don't let yourself become a doormat, of course. But don't wait for other people to fill your life with positive energy, either. Instead, take the lead and be the positive influence for others that you wish they would be for you.

Imagine I dropped you off on Michigan Avenue one Saturday morning and asked you to walk a mile without saying hello to anyone. When you got to the end of that mile, how many people do you think would have said hello to you? Zero. Now, imagine we went back on Sunday and I dropped you in the same spot. But *this* time, you made it a point to greet everyone you saw. Now, tell me, how many people do you think would've said hello to you by the end of *that* mile-long walk down Michigan Ave.? I guarantee you that number would be a whole lot higher than zero.

The business guru and motivational speaker Zig Ziglar once said, "You can have everything in life you want if you just help enough other people get what they want." Call it a variation on the Golden Rule: you get what you give in life. It's so simple. Everybody gets it. Treat other people how you want to be treated. Dole out positivity; get positivity in return. Lie, cheat, steal, and stab others in the back; expect to get lied to, cheated on, stolen from, and betrayed more than once in your life. There's no getting around it: the universe won't give us a thing unless we give first.

Conclusion

Adversity is coming for you in the same way it has for me and every other successful person in the world. Make your peace with that fact now. More importantly, prepare yourself for it, when the trials come, you won't fold under the pressure. Instead, you'll be ready with a bulletproof mindset and a handful of options to throw at the problem at hand. Will you screw up? Yes, you will. Will you fail? Sometimes, but the truth is this: you're only a failure if you *don't* get yourself up off the mat. So, next time you face adversity, remember it's a normal part of the process. Take your licks, try on different solutions, get up, and keep moving forward. Adversity will teach you more than a book like this one ever could. Own it and be ready to learn.

CHAPTER 03

Where I Come From

> **IT** DOESN'T MATTER WHERE
> YOU COME FROM. IT'S WHAT
> YOU DO WHEN YOU GET HERE.
>
> MALCOLM BUTLER

Every entrepreneur has a story to tell. For some, family money, trust funds, and corporate connections play an outsized role. For others, humble roots and bootstraps mark their journey from rags to riches. For me, that story begins in the humble Midwest. I didn't grow up with money in the bank, and the only funds I could trust in were the few dollars my family scraped together through hard work. Does that make my story any more legitimate than anyone else's? Absolutely not. If you've got a pile of money and an idea to run with, then all the more power to you. But, most of us *don't* start with the deck stacked in our favor. For too many would-be entrepreneurs, that lack of a head-start gives them just enough of an excuse to never get started at all.

In this chapter, I want to share my story—not so you can see how great I am or anything like that. Rather, I want you to see that it doesn't matter *where* you start or *what* your past looks like. You don't need to have been born with a silver spoon in your mouth, and you certainly don't need a hereditary link to the business world in order to get your foot in the door. If you're willing to do the work, then even the humblest background can serve as a jumping-off point for your future success. I hope my origin story serves as just one example of why that's true.

Tracing My Small Town Roots

I was raised in Kennett, Missouri. With a population just north of 10,000 and a median household income of around $20,000 to $25,000, you could definitely call Kennett a small town. My parents were too busy fighting with each other to keep up with me as a kid, so I found plenty of ways to get into trouble. Hiding in ditches with friends and pitching water balloons at passing cars on the highway was one of my favorite ways to pass time. With a childhood like mine, it's a wonder I didn't end up in jail.

Growing up, I had an uncle who owned a large tract of land near the border between Arkansas and Missouri. When I was young, he'd drop me off in the cotton fields and I'd spend the day "chopping cotton." Walking up and down the half-mile rows, I'd root, cut, and rearrange weeds so that they wouldn't choke out the cotton or gum up the combine. For 13 hours a day, I toiled under the hot summer sun with no iPhone or Walkman to keep me company. All I carried was a garden hoe, a cooler full of water, and a bologna sandwich for lunch. It was brutal but, for four bucks an hour, I was game.

When I got old enough to lift something heavier than a garden hoe, I started pitching watermelons—not at cars, but onto a trailer. What we'd do is take four guys and walk beside a trailer as a pickup truck pulled it slowly through a family friend's watermelon fields. One by one, a guy would roll each watermelon to see if it was ready, tear it off, and pitch it to the next guy over. His job would be to pass it on to the "bumper," who'd toss it down the bed of the truck to the "stacker." He'd catch and stack the watermelons into a neat pyramid so that they wouldn't roll off the trailer.

I was usually the stacker, so it was my job to catch the playing watermelons. We had a slick operation; the watermelons came fast and, if you weren't paying attention, you'd get clobbered. The other guys I worked with usually made a game of chucking the melons at me—their way of picking on the little kid. As much as they gave me a hard time, I learned some valuable lessons from those guys and our time in the fields. You can never take honest work for granted, and there's something uniquely fulfilling about working hard to get the job done. You could say the cotton and watermelon fields are where I picked up the work ethic that's driven me to where I am today. Still, at the end of each day, I felt like death. I knew I could do this kind of work for a while, but the farmer's life couldn't be my long-term future.

Losing my Home

As you may have guessed by now, I've been working hard for my entire life. But work was about more than earning a few bucks to blow on comic books and video games. When my parents divorced at age 13, my brother and I stuck with our dad in the house we had grown up in. At that time, he owned a salvage yard, a detail shop, and was working as a manager at Kroger. All at once, though, a Walmart Supercenter came to town and put my dad's Kroger out of business, his top mechanic quit for a job at Nucor, and the detail shop folded. Soon after those three streams of income dried up, we defaulted on our mortgage and lost the house. In what seemed like the blink of an eye, everything had vanished.

Losing our home was devastating, to say the least. Everything changed almost immediately. People who'd been in our lives seemed to become more distant. A few friends I'd grown up with weren't as interested in spending time with me as before. When things were going well for my parents, it was like we were at the top of the food chain in our small town. Now, when everything had fallen apart, our reality became very different. Eventually, my dad would pick up another job working at the new Walmart for $9 an hour. From business owner to Walmart associate—we were all just a little bit humbled.

The work ethic I'd picked up on my uncle's farm paid dividends during this season. I was just 14 at this point, so I started working under the table in a little steakhouse. I'd get out of school and go straight to work for the night. I even worked on weekends—whatever I had to do to play my part. When I turned 15, I grabbed a learner's permit and took over my dad's $250-a-month car payment. It wasn't exactly legal, but driving that car to and from work allowed me to pack even more hours into my already-crammed schedule. We needed the money, so that's what I did.

Broken Legs and Repaired Relationships

Things eventually worked out for us. We managed to put a roof over our heads and food on the table. And, in a twist I never saw coming, my father even ended up marrying a woman who'd played a crucial role in my childhood. To tell that story, though, I have to back up a few years into my own. As a kid, I was always a strong athlete. I killed it on the soccer field but was good at plenty of other sports too. But all that came to a crashing halt in middle school. One day after football practice, two kids got into a fight and, somehow, one of them managed to fall onto my left knee and break it in half. That night, I was supposed to march in the town's annual parade to celebrate my little league team's recent trip to regionals (like I said, I played a lot of sports). That parade was one of my favorite nights of the year. But, instead of marching up Main Street, I got to spend the night in an operating room.

The prognosis wasn't good: I'd broken a growth plate in my left leg and needed to wear a cast from my thigh to my ankle for several months. It was a difficult time for me, but one of the bright spots in that process was a physical therapist named Sharon. She was really nice, super sweet, and very quiet—the opposite of what I experienced in my turbulent childhood home. Sharon walked me through some of my deepest struggles in recovery, especially towards what I *thought* would be the end.

Just as I was able to think about playing sports again, an x-ray revealed that my growth plate hadn't healed as it should. If things continued to grow on their current trajectory, my doctor said, I'd end up with a crooked leg. Long story short, the "fix" involved a specialist from St. Louis drilling out the growth plate above both my knees. Thanks to that procedure, I lost four inches of growth and effectively skipped that growth spurt every teenager is supposed to hit in high school. 16 years old, 5 feet tall, and barely over 100 pounds, I felt (and looked) like a little kid roaming the halls of my school. That's when I realized I would never make it as a professional athlete. There was just no shot.

Through all that, Sharon was there. She was there to guide me through the physical challenges of recovery. She was also there to help me process the emotional struggles of putting my dreams to bed and trying to navigate high school as a pipsqueak. She became a friend to me—one I desperately needed in that rough season. In the process, she got to know my dad as well. They dated and eventually, they got married. In all, I came to love Sharon truly as if she were my mother. None of that is meant to take anything away from my biological mother, of course. She was in my life, too, and without her care and support, I would've been lost. After all, *she* was the one who drove me to and from my appointments with Sharon. To this day, both women hold a tremendous amount of influence in my life.

Saying No to Kennett and Yes to Chicago

Sharon did more than just help me deal with the injury I suffered as a child. She became a catalyst for who I'd become as an adult. For much of my young life, I stayed firmly planted in Kennett. Even though I'd briefly visited places like Memphis and Colorado a few times, 99.5% of my experience was in small-town Missouri. So, when Sharon brought us up to Chicago to visit her family, words can't describe what I experienced there in the big city.

In my wildest dreams, I never imagined such a place as Chicago. The buildings, the people, the number of things to do *besides* toss water balloons at cars—everything about the city grabbed me by the eyeballs and refused to let go. From that moment, I knew what I had to do. Farming ran deep in my roots, but the prospect of working long, lonely days out in a field had always sounded like torture to me. There was a new city—really, a new world—out there for me to uncover in Chicago. So, once high school was over and I was free to move on, I packed my bags and headed for the Windy City.

Later on, I'll have more to say about Chicago, college, and the birth of what would one day become Ultimate Team Products. But before I can go on about what the city's done for me, I need to give Kennett it's due. I don't regret leaving my small town; it's what I needed to do. But to say I wanted something *more* out of life than Kennett could offer isn't to say *less* about my hometown. There's a lot I appreciate and miss about my small-town upbringing. Life was simpler in wonderful ways—not the least of which include the expenses of living in a small town vs. the big city. Kennett made me; there are people and places there that will always hold a special place in my heart. There's no getting past my roots; without them, I wouldn't be who I am.

Conclusion

When I coach younger people, I often hear them romanticize about "getting out" of their current situation the same way I "got out" of Kennett. They think that once they get beyond the social and cultural limitations of their hometown, they'll find some kind of absolute freedom out there in the wide, wide world. But reality never works like that. Whenever you leave a place, you inevitably bring one crucial thing with you: *yourself.* No matter where you go, you'll attract people a circle of people who know your business just as intimately in a big city as they would if you lived in a small town. Unless you actively work to cultivate that circle in positive directions, you'll encounter all the same social constraints you would've dealt with if you'd never left home. You'll be the same person surrounded by the same kinds of people, just in a new place.

You can't "get out" of your story; the people and places who made you will forever impact who you are and what you bring to your business. None of that means that your future is determined by your past. Your story is still *your* story. The future will be what you make of it. You can never change where you come from, but where you're going is completely up to you. So, take some time to remember who you are and where you come from, but don't take too long. The pen is in your hand, and it's up to you to write whatever comes next.

Before You Get Started in Business

> **IF** YOU DON'T KNOW WHERE
> YOU'RE GOING, YOU'LL END UP
> SOMEPLACE ELSE.
>
> YOGI BERRA

CHAPTER 04

magine you're standing in a big, empty room with four corners: A, B, C, and D. Suddenly, you hear a voice say, "Pick a corner and go there." So, you decide to indulge the voice and head towards Corner A. As you're strolling in that direction, a giant boulder drops out of nowhere and blocks your path. "Forget that," you think, and start making your way towards Corner B. On your way there, though, a chair comes flying across the room and lands between you and your corner. Once again, you shift course and head over to Corner C. This time, you start running. But before you can pick up enough steam, a gap opens in the floor. Left with one option, you head over to Corner D.

Now, go back to the beginning and imagine the voice one more time. This time, instead of giving you an option, the voice says, "There's a million dollars sitting in a briefcase over in Corner A." Immediately, you put your head down and start trucking. The boulder falls, but you're on a mission, so you sidestep the huge rock and keep going towards your destination. The chair comes flying, but you duck it. The gap opens, but you long jump the gap before it can get too wide. Before you know it, you've reached your destination. You had to get creative, of course. You had to duck, dodge, and dive in all kinds of ways you couldn't possibly have anticipated. But you made it. Why? Because you set your sights on a target and you made it your mission to get there.

Out of the Room and into the Business World

When I talk to high school students and young adults about entrepreneurship, I often walk them through something like the exercise I shared above. The one thing I want to convey to them is the importance of intentionality and vision when you're starting a business. The typical entrepreneurship story looks like the first paragraph I shared above. Entrepreneur Bob comes up with an idea and takes off in a direction—*any* direction—hoping for success. Obstacles emerge and setbacks happen, so he shifts course and starts heading for another corner. Before long, though, Bob starts to feel like he's drifting. He started out without any idea where he was going, and now he's landed exactly where Yogi said he would: "someplace else." Bob's lost, tired, and demoralized, so he finally decides to hang up his entrepreneur hat and get a real job.

But what if Bob's story looked a lot more like the second paragraph I shared above? What if Bob heard a voice—*his* voice—and it told him that what he wanted most in life (money, success, recognition, etc.) was waiting for him in Corner A. Sure, all the same obstacles and setbacks would get in his way but, instead of changing course, he'd knuckle down and find a way to keep moving towards his mark. In real life, of course, his final destination would look a whole lot different than he originally envisioned. But here's the most important part: he'd get *there* instead of someplace else.

Unless you want to end up six miles wide of Corner D, looking for an entry-level gig at the local Lego factory, you need to start your business with a strong sense of where you want to take it and how you think you'll get there. Sure, you can only know so much about the journey before you actually set foot on the path, but that's not a good reason to start wandering aimlessly. In the rest of this chapter, then, I'm going to help you think about where you want to go and how to chart a path from here to there. But first, we need to stop and talk about why you're even considering the hard slog of entrepreneurship.

Start With Why

In 2014, an author and organizational consultant named Simon Sinek gave what would go on to become the third most popular TED talk of all time: "Start with Why." In it, Sinek explained the secret to inspirational leadership. From Martin Luther King Jr. to Steve Jobs, he said, the most effective leaders in the world haven't been the ones who lead with *what* but those who lead with *why*. MLK didn't change the world by scolding people into treating each other better. Instead, he appealed to the deeper *why* of civil rights—everyone's built-in sense of equality. Steve Jobs didn't make Apple the tech giant it is by constantly pointing at how awesome their products were. Instead, he invited us all to join him as he challenged the status quo in consumer electronics.

Ask any decent salesman and they'll tell you: people won't give a rip about *what* you're selling until you convince them *why* they should care. As a business owner, you'll have to engage in sales on multiple levels. Obviously, you're going to have to sell your product or service to customers. Beyond that, you'll constantly have to sell your vision to team members and prospective hires as you try to inspire them to make your business go. If you decide to raise funds, get ready to put on your best sales pitch to prospective investors.

Most important of all, though, you'll have to sell the business to yourself each and every day. When the excitement fades and the realities of building a business set in, you're going to wonder why in the world you signed up for all this. Trust me; there are going to be days when all you want to do is give up and get a "real" job. Friends will stab you in the back. Partners will cut you out. Suppliers will put the screws to you. You'll fail, you'll fall, and you'll want nothing more than to run and hide. On those dark days, you'd better have a strong reason *why* you started down this road. If you don't, you just might listen to that little voice when it calls you to take the easy way out and quit.

So, why are you doing this? Why do you want to be an entrepreneur? Why do you want to build a business? If you've got a specific product in mind, why *this* product and why should anyone care? What are you trying to change in the world? Whose lives are supposed to benefit from your success? Why are you willing to put yourself through the entrepreneurial wringer? If you haven't taken the time to search your soul, now's the time. Start with why, and you'll give yourself exactly what you need to survive the long journey ahead.

Begin With the End in Mind

Now that you've taken some time to think about where you're

coming from, it's time to think more about where you're going. What's your endgame? Where do you want this thing to go? Do you want to build something incredible that you can pass on to your kids? Or, do you want to get in, make some money, and then get out? For plenty of entrepreneurs today, that's the plan: build a profitable business, sell it, and then move on to the next thing. That's a fine strategy, and with stories coming out every day about some 24-year-old selling his business to Google for $100 million, selling is definitely an attractive thing to do. If that's where you are, then everything I'm about to say about beginning with the end in mind is going to be crucial to your success.

But even if you're like me and you never want to let your company go, you still need to build it like you plan to sell it. If I could go back and change anything about the early days of UTP, that would be it. When you go to sell a business, there are certain things a buyer needs to see: organized sales data, all contracting and legal paperwork, robust contact databases, clearly documented systems. Here's the thing: all of that is crucial to running an efficient business *regardless of whether you plan to sell.* When I started, I didn't have a system for keeping up with any of that stuff because I never anticipated having to hand off the business. If I'd begun with the end in mind, then I would've dialed those things in from day one. Because I didn't, I often find myself having to go back and retrofit basic systems and processes—even to this very day.

If I had to go back and do it over, I would've started building a contact database from the beginning. I would've documented *everything* and made sure to keep all our legal ducks in a row. I would've gamed out personnel decisions and thought more carefully about the kind of people I'd need on my team. If you don't know how to do any of that right now, don't worry. I'll flesh these things out as we get deeper into the book. For now, suffice it to say that if I knew how important all this stuff was on the front end, I would have done it. Now, you do. So, don't cut corners just because you never want to sell. If you follow my advice and build something that *can* be sold, I guarantee you won't want to.

The Man With a Plan?

Now that you've thought about the *why* and the *where*, it's time to consider *how* you plan to build your business. Business planning is a double-edged sword. On the one side, there's real value in thinking through your idea, doing detailed market research, and writing everything out in a comprehensive plan. Especially if you're going after a small business administration (SBA) loan or you're looking to raise funds with serious investors, people are going to need to see your plan in writing. On the other side of the sword, though, business planning can cut a would-be entrepreneur down before she even gets started. Why? Because writing a plan assumes you need to *know* a lot more than is possible before you actually get to work. For new entrepreneurs, the tendency with planning is to spend so much time on it that you never actually get to the part where you build the business.

Here's what I think: writing an in-depth business plan is *usually* an exercise in putting the cart before the horse. Want to launch a t-shirt business? Instead of sitting in your room for 40 hours and working out a detailed plan based on hypotheticals about what you *think* will happen, print up a couple of shirts, get out there, and sell them. Start small, make a few mistakes, and build out your supply chain. Listen to your customers and learn how to sell. *Then*, you can sit down and write up a simple plan based on what you've learned in the real world.

What to Include in Your Business Plan

Strictly speaking, there's no right or wrong way to write a business plan. What matters most is that the plan meets your specific needs. For most startups, a simple plan like what I mentioned above will be best. Drawing on material from the Small Business Administration (SBA), here are the key elements of a simple startup business plan:

- **Partnerships** - What sorts of vendors, suppliers, and services will you tap to make your business go? Give an account of the players on your field, making sure to specify where you've already built strategic partnerships and how you plan to leverage them for the good of your business.

- **Activities** - What's your core offering and what sort of business will you be engaged in? Be sure to specify how your offering meets a need in the market.

- **Unique Value Proposition** - Your value proposition expresses how you plan to meet the market's needs in a way that sets you apart from all of your competitors. Whether it's price, quality, or service, be sure your plan conveys what makes your company worth investing in over against all the rest.

- **Resources** - What sorts of tools do you have in your kit? Think in terms of your personal expertise, existing intellectual property, and staff resources. Example: if you're getting into software development and your primary developer spent a decade at Google, say so.

- **Customer Relationships** - What will the typical buying experience look like from first-contact through sale to customer service and beyond? Will they interact with you, your sales force, your website, or some other means? Think small here, detailing the steps it takes to convert interest into action and how to leverage current relationships for new business in the future.

- **Customer Segments** - Who are you trying to reach? What do they look like? Where do they live? How do they think? Where will they make contact with you and your product? Don't try to cast too wide a net here. If you try to reach everybody, you'll end up reaching nobody.

- **Channels** - Where do you plan to reach your customers? Social media? Print advertising? Word of mouth? In person? Specify your marketing channels and how you plan to utilize them.

- **Cost Structure** - Quantity or quality? Would you rather sell a ton of products for a low price or just a few for much more? Lay out your cost structure in terms of production and sales, paying special attention to cost margins.

- **Revenue Streams** - How will you make money: product sales, royalties, commissions, memberships? Specify the exact ways in which revenue will flow into your company.

Whether you're looking for a small business loan or you're raising money from individual investors, some people are going to want to see more than a simple startup plan can offer. In that case, below are what SBA considers the main elements of a traditional plan. Keep in mind: this type of plan involves a ton of up-front work and can end up running more than 10 pages long. So, reserve this kind of in-depth work for *after* you've gotten your feet wet and got a good sense of what's what in your industry.

- **Executive Summary** - This opening summary should lay out a concise description of your company as well as its core offering, mission statement, and current high-level personnel structure. Include a snapshot of your current financial information and plans for future growth as well.

- **Company Description** - Your description should offer a detailed account of the partners, activities, value proposition, and resources laid out above. This is where you get to make an emotional connection, so be sure to tell the story in a way that describes the need in the market as you see it and your unique capacity to fill it.

- **Market Analysis** - Dig up industry benchmark and potential competitors' performance data. What are they doing that works? What are they doing that doesn't work? Do you see any trends in the market that your product or service is uniquely positioned to tap into? Whether you plan to pitch your business plan to potential investors or not, this kind of information will be invaluable in helping you build a business that actually wins in the marketplace.

- **Organization & Management** - Here's where you get into the organizational structure of your company. First of all, specify whether you plan to incorporate and how (C- or S- corporation, general or limited partnership, sole proprietor or LLC). Next, build out your organizational chart. For each person on your team, describe their expertise and experience, as well as how it helps the business.

- **Service or Product** - What are you selling and why should people buy it? Build on the activities, unique value proposition, and customer relationships items in the simple startup plan (above) in order to show what exactly you plan to bring to the market and what the customer's experience with it will look like from start to finish. If your product development involves research, patents, and intellectual property considerations, be sure to include that information in your plan.

- **Marketing & Sales** - Again, building on some of the items I shared above (customer relationships, segments, and channels), use this section to sketch out your initial marketing plan. Your strategy will grow and evolve as your business does, but you need an initial plan showing that you not only know where your customers are but that you have a good sense of how you'll go out and get them.

- **Funding Request** - If you're looking to raise funds, this is where you specify precisely what you need and what you're willing to give up in return (debt or equity). Be sure to say what you plan to do with the money, whether that's investing in equipment, materials, or human capital. If you plan to sell the business in the future, outline the path that'll get you there. If you're looking for financing, specify your strategy for paying off that debt as well as specific terms.

- **Financial Projections** - Project out your anticipated performance over the short-term (6 months), medium-term (1 year), and long-term (5 years). Include as much supporting documentation as you can (income and cash flow statements, tax returns, budgets, etc.). Especially if you're looking for funding, these projections should convince potential investors why your business is a smart bet.

Lost yet? Don't worry. If all that stuff about C-corporations and organizational charts sounds foreign to you, just hang with me. As we go on with these practical lessons, we'll get deeper into the essential stuff you need to know to start your business.

Conclusion

"Why do I want to start this business and where do I want it to go?" Those are two of the most important questions any budding entrepreneur can ask him- or herself. They're not easily answered, and it usually takes a whole lot of soul searching and visualizing to figure out precisely what's motivating you to take this plunge. But if you'll do that hard work now, it'll pay dividends in the future. The world will drop boulders in your path, hurl chairs at you from across the room, and open up sinkholes as wide as the Grand Canyon—all to keep you from reaching your destination. Own that reality and convince yourself *now* that the journey is worth every hassle that comes your way. Do that, and you'll find the strength you need to put your head down and keep moving forward.

CHAPTER 05

It All Started in My Dorm Room

" WHEN YOU FIND AN IDEA THAT YOU JUST
CAN'T STOP THINKING ABOUT, THAT'S
PROBABLY A GOOD ONE TO PURSUE.

JOSH JAMES, CO-FOUNDER AND CEO OF
OMNITURE, FOUNDER, AND CEO OF DOMO

B y the time *Batman Begins* hit the theaters in 2005, the world had already seen 6 movies featuring the caped crusader on the big screen—not to mention the live-action and animated series on TV. Still, the seventh installment in the Batman franchise ended up grossing $373 million worldwide and kicking off a veritable renaissance in superhero flicks. Why all the excitement over a movie about a character who'd been around since 1939? Here's my theory: it was the allure of a good origin story. It didn't matter that we'd seen Batman plenty of times already; we were willing to pay $12 to see him reborn.

Origin stories are inherently fascinating. Whenever someone we admire says they're going to tell us their story, we shut up and listen. Stories about Steve Jobs building computers in his garage or Phil Knight selling shoes out of his trunk grab our attention. Why? Because they don't just tell us where someone or something is coming from; they get right down on our level and invite us to imagine our *own* possibilities. If Jobs could launch something like Apple out of a garage, so could I. If Knight could turn his shoe-peddling into a global enterprise, so could I. If Bruce Wayne could put on a mask and a cape... well, maybe not that one.

In this chapter, I want to tell you the story of how UTP was born. I get it; I'm no Phil Knight and our business isn't anywhere near Nike. But stories like the one I'm about to tell are important to all of us because, for every Jobs or Knight, there are thousands of entrepreneurs like me who've taken a solid idea and turned it into a multimillion dollar business. You'll never see their names in lights or read about their stories in Forbes, but they're living the entrepreneurial dream. If you want to know what it looks like to launch a business, ask one of us. Odds are, our story will sound a whole lot more real to you than that of a one-in-a-million like Jobs. I'm hoping you come away from *this* real story of entrepreneurship and say, "If *he* can do it, then so could I."

Chicago: The Town that Called Me Home

In chapter 3, I shared the story of my small-town upbringing and eventual decision to leave for Chicago. The truth is, if it weren't for my stepmother, Sharon, and her family, I never could've made such a dramatic move. Growing up, I never really knew what it was like to have grandparents. My dad's mom died shortly after giving birth to him. His father couldn't take care of him, so his mother's parents adopted him soon after birth. My mom's parents died when I was really young. With Sharon in the picture, though, I inherited a grandmother who loved me like I was her own. If she hadn't lived in Chicago, I never would've seen the city for myself—at least, not at that point in my life. And if I didn't know she was close by, I don't think I could've brought myself to finally make the move.

Sharon's mom lived in the suburban city of Berwyn. Trying to stay as close to her as I could, I made it a point to tour Dominican University in nearby River Forest. I instantly fell in love. The community feel of the university and its neighborhood appealed to the small-town Midwesterner in me—all without straying much more than 10 miles from downtown Chicago. On top of that, the historic homes in that neighborhood were unlike anything I'd ever seen. Something in me thought that by immersing myself in a neighborhood like that, some of its class would rub off on me. So, in the fall of 2002, I enrolled at Dominican and moved into Coughlin Hall.

Retired at 30... Why Not?

It didn't take long for Dominican to uncover my entrepreneurial drive. In fact, one of my first class experiences made it abundantly clear what track my life would take. The classroom was full of anxious freshmen and the professor—Dr. Calabrese—decided to break the ice by asking each of us where we'd like to be professionally by the time we turned 30. When he got to me, I piped up confidently, "Retired." Not a few kids in the class snickered as Calabrese followed up, "Really? Ok. Let's say you actually achieve your goals and retire at the age of 30. What comes next? And before you say something like 'buy stuff and travel,' let's say you give yourself two years to get all that out of your system. So, you've traveled the world for two years, gone everywhere you've wanted to go, seen everything you've wanted to see, bought everything you've wanted to buy, and done everything you've always wanted to do. Then what? You're 32; now what are you going to do with your life?"

I didn't know it then, but Dr. Calabrese would become one of my favorite professors and a man who, to this day, I look to for advice. I don't remember what I said to him in that classroom, but the honest truth was I didn't have an answer to his question. That afternoon, I went back to my dorm room to reflect more deeply on it. That's when I realized something. It wasn't so much that I wanted to *be* retired; I just wanted the option. I wanted the control that comes from paving your own way. I didn't want to be chained to a desk or locked into a career I didn't love. I wanted to be free.

To this day, that hasn't changed. I'm well past 30, but I'm nowhere close to being done. In fact, I'm not sure I ever will retire—not because I'm like the majority of people in America who *can't* retire on their current level of savings. No, I don't *want* to retire. Why? Because I've learned to work right. Just as importantly, I've created a place where other people can come and work right as well. And when you're working on something you love and believe in alongside other people who love and believe in it as well, retirement isn't something you look forward to or even really think about all that much. Instead, you're glad to be at work and grateful for every day you get to spend building your dream.

What Else Happened in that Dorm Room?

You could say that first class primed the pump and got me thinking in the right direction: "If I want to be the master of my own destiny by the time I turn 30, how am I going to get there?" The beginning of an answer to that question snuck up on me one day when I wasn't looking. My brother's baseball team, the Holcomb Hornets, had made it to the state tournament, and I wanted to do something nice for him and my mom. So,

I asked my friend—a graphic design major—if he could help me doctor up a photo of my brother's team. I didn't want anything complicated. All we did was take a photo of the team, blur the background, lay it out, and have it printed. Without thinking much of it, I sent the "poster" to my mom. Right away, she asked if I could print up one for each remaining kid on the team. There it was; without even trying, I had my first order.

Right away, I thought I was on to an idea worth exploring. I sat down with my friend to strategize and, from there, came up with a whole bunch of different avenues to pursue. For one of our first attempts, he and I tried visiting basketball courts in inner city Chicago and taking photos of kids on the court. We did our best to determine who the best player was and then printed out a free photo for him, hoping his friends would catch on and buy one for themselves. Yeah right. It was a clever idea, but we sold exactly zero photos that way. Something had to change if my business idea was going to get legs.

Fake it Till You Make It

About the time our new business—MSP Designs—was getting off the ground, my friend and I worked at J Alexander's in Oakbrook, IL. One day, I told one of my regulars about the new business. As it turns out, he directed a local baseball tournament and thought it'd be a great idea for me to come down and see if I could sell a few posters. It was a 5-day event: Wednesday through Friday in the evenings and all day Saturday and Sunday. I was terrified and excited at the same time. We were still in a dorm room at this point with just a couple of computers, no printers, and pretty much no clue what we were actually doing. So, of course, I said yes.

We may not have known what we were doing, but we weren't about to let that stop us. After spending Wednesday, Thursday, and Friday night on the field snapping photos of the teams in the tournament, my friend and I stayed up all night graphically enhancing the photos into awesome posters (the same work our design team does today). Then, we had a local shop in Chicago print them out for us to use in our display. The plan was to label each photo with a letter of the alphabet. Of course, there were more teams (33) than letters. Call that amateur move #1. Amateur move # 2 came when we taped each photo to a hacked up piece of cardboard and displayed them out on a "rented" folding table from Home Depot. It only took about 10 minutes and a light gust of wind for all our photos to take flight.

Just imagine two college kids bolting across a field trying to run down their display photos and *then* trying to convince everybody that we knew what we were doing. And that's not even *half* of the rookie mistakes we made at that first event. Still, amateur hour or not, we ended up turning a healthy profit that weekend. That's not bad for a couple of kids with no experience and little more than an idea.

Taking the Next Step

When I talk to teenagers and young adults about entrepreneurship, one of the most common questions I hear is this: what made you decide to move forward with your idea? First and foremost, the business *excited* me. After that first event, I couldn't remember getting that amped about anything in my entire life. From that day forward, my thoughts were consumed by the laundry list of problems we'd encountered and what I could do to solve them creatively. To be honest, the thought that it could all fail didn't even cross my mind. Instead, I found myself thinking about the business day and night, strategizing about how we'd get new customers and grow the business into something substantial. I had finally found something that set my soul on fire. When you find something that captivates your interest and creativity like that, you're crazy not to at least pursue it. So, that's what I decided to do.

I'd be lying if I said the prospect of working for myself didn't play a huge role in my decision to go all-in on the business. I'd mostly had great jobs over the years and got to work for some wonderful people. But I'd come to discover that, as much as people may genuinely believe they have your best interests at heart, everybody's favorite radio station is still WIIFM: What's In It For Me. Your boss may be kind and generous, but they've ultimately got a responsibility to themselves and their business—regardless of what that might mean for you and your livelihood. I never wanted to find myself in a position where somebody else held that kind of control over me. So, I decided to build a company. 15 years, 2 continents, and more than 130 team members later, I'm confident I made the right choice.

The True Value of College

Full disclosure: I never graduated from Dominican. I quit with 1 semester of class left. Why? It may seem petty, but I believed I was on to something with MSP and I didn't want the school to somehow take credit for what I'd built with my own blood and sweat because, truth be told, there aren't many classes that can teach you how to build a company. By that point, I'd had already been skipping most of my weekday classes to work with a local roofing company, always looking for capital to get my business off the ground. In a lot of ways, that job taught me more than those classes ever could. The owner, Willie Fellows, became one of my favorite mentors in business. Just like the guys I'd pitched watermelons with in Kennett, Willie embodied the value of a strong work ethic. That's exactly what I needed as I was busting my tail trying to launch my business.

Does all that mean Dominican was a waste of time? Definitely not. I already mentioned Dr. Calabrese and how his gentle nudging set me down the path to entrepreneurship. Another teacher who had a profound impact on me was one of my business professors, Arvid Johnson. In my first class with Professor Johnson, I took a look at his syllabus and noticed that you could get a maximum of 1,000 points in the class for attendance, assignments, quizzes, etc. So, the first thing I did was walk up to him and say, "I looked at your syllabus and just wanted to let you know that, as soon as I get 700 points, I'm not coming back to class." He laughed me off but, sure enough, I got my 700 points and just stopped going. I didn't even take the final. Why bother?

Professor Johnson and I ended up becoming friends after that. When I brought him my idea for MSP, he was gracious, but I know he wasn't impressed. I'm sure he didn't think I was going anywhere. Really, who could blame him? Regardless, he gave me a piece of advice that's stuck with me to this day: my true competitive advantage would be in my network of and relationship with tournament directors—not my product. In the coming chapters, I'll flesh out the importance of network-building. For now, suffice it to say that Professor Johnson showed me that the most valuable asset I have in business is the bundle of connections I'm able to forge with tournament directors, partners, and team members. At one level, I'd always known that, but he gave me the push I needed to focus my creative energy on building and maintaining relationships with people as a way to build my business. Little nuggets of wisdom like that are the most valuable thing I took with me from Dominican.

Conclusion

In the coming chapters, I'll have much more to say about the early days of my business. I'm only a little embarrassed to say that the tournament experience I described above only scratches the surface of all the mistakes we made along the way. Crazy stories are good, though, not just for their entertainment value but for the valuable lessons they teach us along the way. As you've already learned, I've spilled a lot of my own blood on the entrepreneurial battleground. Thankfully, you don't have to repeat my mistakes. But before we can get into all the gory details, we need to stop for a moment to consider the practical realities of opening up your own business. To those, we turn in the next chapter.

How to Get Started

> "THE CRITICAL INGREDIENT IS GETTING OFF YOUR BUTT AND DOING SOMETHING. IT'S AS SIMPLE AS THAT. A LOT OF PEOPLE HAVE IDEAS, BUT THERE ARE FEW WHO DECIDE TO DO SOMETHING ABOUT THEM NOW. NOT TOMORROW. NOT NEXT WEEK. BUT TODAY. THE TRUE ENTREPRENEUR IS A DOER, NOT A DREAMER.
>
> NOLAN BUSHNELL, FOUNDER OF ATARI

Imagine we chartered a jet and spent the next week hopping from continent to continent looking for one thing: McDonald's French Fries. On Monday morning, we'd find a pair of golden arches in London. That afternoon, we'd move on to Paris. Later that evening, we'd hit Amsterdam. And so on. Here's what would happen. Making exceptions for language and culture, I guarantee our experience in every one of those McDonald's would be virtually identical. From the front door to our first bite, everything would fit the chain's meticulously-constructed mold. It wouldn't matter whether the Japanese man who took our order just had the worst day of his life or the Chilean woman on the deep fryer just had her best. McDonald's has dialed in the entire process to produce *one* consistent outcome across all tribes, tongues, and nations: a red sleeve filled with perfectly-crisped straws of golden perfection.

McDonald's is one of the classic examples of scale in business. When the legendary Ray Kroc took over franchising from the original McDonald brothers, he inherited a great product and developed a process to get it into the hands of people all over the world. While it helps that the early McDonald's could make delicious burgers and fries on the cheap, what made all the difference was Kroc's ability to consistently reproduce that product in every single franchise. If every time you hit a McDonald's, you had no idea whether they'd hand you golden, delicious fries or a floppy, soggy mess, then you'd probably find another fast-food joint to eat at.

Kroc seems to confirm the old chestnut, "with a good enough plan, you can sell anything." I wouldn't go quite that far, but the insight is true enough. Planning and process are at least, if not more, important than the product itself. Who knows how many world-changing products have never penetrated the market for the simple reason that their creators couldn't *sell* their creations. What Kroc and McDonald's demonstrate is the importance of process and structure in amplifying the reach of your products and services—whether it's graphic design, software development, or french fries. In this chapter, I'm going to help you build the foundation for that kind of structure.

Don't Waste Time on Stuff That Doesn't Matter Right Now

Too many would-be entrepreneurs fall in love with the idea of building their own company and then flame out before they ever make their first sale. Why? More often than not, the problem is "paralysis of analysis." Young entrepreneurs feel like there's just so much to do—writing plans, designing logos, developing web sites, forging partnerships, drawing up contracts, etc.—before they can even think about launching their business. As a result, they end up spending all their money and energy on the right things at the wrong time. If they're persistent enough, they'll take a needlessly long road to success. If they're not, they'll just give up and go home.

Take logos, for example. New entrepreneurs often think that if they can spend enough time on it, they'll design the next iconic logo à la FedEx, Nike, or Adidas. Here's what they forget: the FedEx logo is a block of text with an arrow hidden in it, Nike is a curvy checkmark, and Adidas is 3 slanted lines. There's nothing special about those logos in themselves. In fact, they're all pretty boring. What matters infinitely more than the logo is the company it represents. These logos are iconic, not because of their design, but because of the brands that stand behind them. They've built products worth buying and have scaled systems to consistently deliver superb quality. These logos "earned" their notoriety on the back of organizational excellence. In the end, logo recognition always follows brand recognition.

You could say the same about graphic and web design as well. I'm a graphic designer by training and trade, so I appreciate great design and a stellar customer experience on the web. What I *don't* appreciate is when business owners use optimization as an excuse for inaction. At the end of the day, toiling over the perfect design is more a matter of pride than it is production. It's like keeping up the paint job on your sports car without ever driving it. Sure, you've got a beautiful machine, but it's not going to get you anywhere by just *looking* pretty. Eventually, you need to put the key in the ignition and shift the thing into drive. The same is true for business.

Ok, So What Really Matters?

In chapters 2 and 4, I focused more on the psychological pieces you'll have to put in place before you could start your business. In this chapter, it's time to get practical. For starters, let's look at the 5 things every entrepreneur needs before they can officially "open" for business:

1. **An Official Entity** - This one seems almost too obvious to say, but at the very least you need a name to get started, even if it's just your own. More than that, you'll need to decide what form your business will take—sole proprietorship, limited liability company, etc. We'll talk more about those options below.

2. **A Logo** - As I said above, you don't want to spend too much time on a logo. There are online services designed to connect you with graphic designers so that you can create your logo quickly and at a minimum of expense. The most popular is 99designs, where you can crowdsource a stellar logo for less than $300.

3. **A Database** - If you don't have a database, you don't have a business. Leads, customers, clients, partners, investors—you need an easy-to-use, centralized way of keeping track of all these people and communicating with them. HubSpot as a free Customer Relationship Management (CRM) platform that will give you everything you need in a database for your first several years in business.

4. **A Way to Pay** - I'll never forget the first time I took a customer's credit card number over the phone. I had no idea what to do with it, but I couldn't tell *him* that. So, I hung up and scrambled to figure it out. Don't put yourself in the same position. Settle your payment processing *before* you get into an embarrassing situation. Thankfully, services like Square and PayPal make taking payment cheaper and easier than it's ever been.

5. **A Bookkeeping Solution** - You've got to track every dollar that enters or exits your business. Unless you want to pay your accountant gobs of cash to sort through boxes of receipts and invoices, get yourself a robust bookkeeping system that manages the whole process. Programs like Zipbooks are simple to use and can even integrate your payment systems (see #4).

Think About Your Legal Structure

When you're just getting started, big words like 'sole proprietorship' and 'incorporation' can sound intimidating. Speaking from personal experience, though, one of the smartest things you can do is take easy, common-sense steps to protect your personal assets in the event that somebody tries to come after your business. In the following, I'll give you a quick rundown of options for structuring your business. Thankfully, websites like LegalZoom have resources and tools for helping you make this decision and execute the appropriate paperwork without wasting time and money.[1]

SOLE PROPRIETORSHIP

The advantage of a sole proprietorship is its simplicity. To operate as a sole proprietor, all you have to do is use your legal name and social security number. The trouble is, a sole proprietorship offers no personal liability protection. As a sole proprietor, you're on the hook for damages resulting

---

[1] I'm not a lawyer and none of this is intended as legal advice. If you have specific questions, I suggest you spend a little time with an attorney. LegalZoom also offers legal consultation for new business owners.

from lawsuits filed by customers or business associates. If a judge were to rule against you in court, they could go after all your assets, including your personal home.

INCORPORATION

There are two types of corporations you can set up: a C-Corp and an S-Corp. Either one offers two important advantages: 1.) personal liability protection; 2.) the ability to borrow funds in the company's name. The disadvantages? In a C-Corp, your income gets taxed at the corporate level and then again at the personal level. In some states, the S-Corp attempts to get around some of that by passing profits and losses through to the company's shareholders.

PARTNERSHIP

Partnerships are a binding arrangement between two or more entities with guidelines for how the business will be run. Since partnerships aren't themselves legal entities, they don't get double-taxed like a corporation. There are two types of partnership: general and limited. General partnerships offer nothing in the way of liability protection. For that, you'd need a limited partnership, which is made up of at least one general partner and then one or more limited partners. As a passive investor, the limited partner is shielded from personal liability judgments as long as they don't participate materially in any part of the business.

LIMITED LIABILITY COMPANY (LLC)

With the liability protection of a corporation and the tax advantages of a partnership, the LLC as the superior choice for businesses at every level. Most people don't realize that Apple, Nike, and Sony, to name just a few, are all structured as LLCs. In most cases, using an LLC will protect your personal assets from any judgments levied against the LLC itself. If the LLC is set up as a pass-through, then you get to enjoy this benefit without having to pay any additional corporate tax. Still, an LLC won't protect your personal assets against every legal judgment. If you fail to keep your personal finances separate from the LLC, a lawyer can "pierce the corporate veil" and come after you in court.

Business Planning, Redux

After your essentials are in place, it's time to get into the market. Unless you're willing to waste a bunch of your time chasing shadows, you'll want to develop a plan. Here, I'm not talking so much about a business plan (see chapter 4) as I am a *strategic* plan. So far, I've had a lot to say about having the end in mind and getting a clear sense of your destination in business. Strategic planning is where we make that more tangible—where we translate vision into action. To that end, here's a simple exercise followed by a couple of examples showing how I use it in my own business.

EXERCISE · BREAK IT DOWN

What's your biggest dream for 5 years from now? Write that dream down and break it into smaller goals. Follow the common SMART acronym to make each goal specific, measurable, achievable, relevant, and time-indexed. Break those goals further down into action steps and start plotting them out on a timeline.

Here's what that exercise looks like from two angles. First, let's say my 5-year dream is to have 100 locations spread across the U.S. I've got about 30 right now, so I need to add 70 over the next 5 years. That means I've got to bring on 14 locations per year—about one per month. With those numbers in mind, I break out a map, look at the cities where we don't have teams, and come up with a prioritized list. I've got a laundry list of steps to take in launching a new location, so I plot those steps out on a timeline for each new city. At that point, I've got all the pieces in place. All that's left is to execute or, more realistically, to delegate much of the work to other members on my team.

Let's look at this process on a shorter time-horizon, this time focusing on revenue targets instead of market penetration. These numbers are just for demonstration, but let's say for the sake of this example I want to clear $3 million in revenue this year. Let's also say that my company averages $100 per team per event. That means we need to make contact with 30,000 teams this year. If we break that down, that's 600 teams per week. Looking at an average of 40 teams per tournament, that means we need to send out 15 crews per week. I could break this down even further, but you get the picture.

Here's the crucial point of this entire exercise: strategic planning is about deciding where you want to end up and then reverse-engineering the process that will get you there. The outcome is a set of specific actions you can take to reach your goals. "Make $3 million" is a fine goal, but there's nothing actionable about it. "Put 15 crews in the field every week," on the other hand, is a concrete *thing* for us to do. It's complex in that it involves a whole list of things that need to happen in our organization, but it's simple in that we've made it second nature. Strictly speaking, we don't *know* how to make $3 million. What we know is how to put crews in the field.

In the same way, you don't *know* how to achieve your biggest goals. If you did, I'd be tempted to say you aren't setting your sights high enough. So, take some time to dream boldly about your 3- to 5-year vision. Then, get your head out of the clouds and reverse-engineer those goals until you come up with component parts you know how to execute. Don't overcomplicate this. Though your operations will eventually get more complex as you continue to grow, the pattern will always be as simple as I've laid out here.

Get to Know Your People

It won't take long before you realize you need help executing your strategic vision. In chapter 5, I mentioned the importance of personal networks in business. I can't stress enough how important it is to take stock of your relationships and how they interface with their business. Later, we'll talk about what that means in terms of investment and fundraising. For now, I'm concerned more with how family and friends can specifically help you operate or market the business.

According to the "Fall 2016 Bank of America Small Business Owner Report," just over 80% of small business owners enlist family members to help support the company (voluntary operational help, personal financing, emotional support, etc.).[2] 53% take it a step further by tapping family members to play an internal role in the business (advisors, employees, partners, etc.). All that to say, it's incredibly common for business owners to pull their personal network into the business. My own team is chock full of people I'm close to, including my wife, mother, sister, and brother-in-law. In fact, nearly every one of my friends is on our payroll.

---

[2] https://smallbiztrends.com/2016/11/family-support-for-entrepreneurs.html

It's important to get intentional about who you'd like to draw into your business. Here's a simple 3-step process for looking at your existing network and deciding who you'd like to pursue intentionally:

1. **Pick 10 People** - Make a list of 10 people you know. Make sure these are people you trust and can see yourself working with in the future.

2. **Chart Their Strengths** - For each name, write down what you think they're good at. Draw from both your relationship and their current job. Where do they excel? More importantly, what do they love to do?

3. **Invite Them In** - Look for areas in your business that could stand to be delegated. Invite people from your list to step in and "lighten your load" on a one-off basis. As they do, assess their work and whether they "fit."

As you walk through this process, it's important to remember that you become who you surround yourself with. Be careful about who you invite into your inner circle and allow to have influence over you and the business. If you're looking for someone to help with bookkeeping, watch how they manage their own finances. If you're looking for a salesperson, don't just look at friends who talk the best game. Watch closely for the ones who show the most discipline. At the heart of this all is the idea that virtue trumps skill every day of the week. Look for the people who have the *qualities* you need in an employee before you let yourself be impressed by their technical skills. At the end of the day, the people you hire will make or break your business. If you hire for virtue, they'll always find a way to do the right thing for you and the business. If you don't, they won't.

The process I've shared in this section is going to look different depending on your product or service, industry, process, and so on. In the broad strokes, though, this is what I've done to figure out which of my friends, family, and acquaintances would make a good member of our team. More than that, I've seen it as an opportunity to give friends opportunities to exercise their talents and discover their true passion. There's nothing like creating a space for people you know and love to discover their wheelhouse, and then letting them loose to flex their unique abilities to help you further grow your business.

Conclusion: Getting By on the Bare Minimum

In business, people often talk about something called the 'minimum viable product' (MVP). Instead of toiling forever to design the perfect widget, they say, you just need to get to the place where your product is "good enough" to ship into the world. After that, you can use customer feedback to tweak and refine future versions of your product. As long as it isn't used as an excuse for poor quality, focusing on your MVP is a good way to keep perfectionism from ruining your business before it even starts.

I know I've shared a lot in this chapter, but what I want more than anything is to help you develop your MVB: minimum viable business. There are so many things you can waste your time on—exquisite logos, intricate structures, tricked-out web design, etc. Don't fall into that trap. Instead, focus on the things that truly matter. Pick a decent name, get yourself a professional logo, set up your database, and line up your payment/bookkeeping services. From there, deconstruct your strategy and then get to work. When you need help, ask for it. Talk to a lawyer or two, but don't think you need to build out a complicated corporate structure *before* you make your first sale.

To wrap it all up in one overly-simplistic bow, the way to get started in business is *to get started in business*. If you take care of the essentials I shared above, you'll be well on your way to multiplying the reach of your product or service and building a consistent operation like McDonald's. There's a lot to do between here and there, but this chapter has already laid the groundwork. In later chapters, I'll have much more to say about what you need to do in order to keep building on that foundation.

The Early Days

"MY BIGGEST MOTIVATION? JUST TO KEEP CHALLENGING MYSELF. I SEE LIFE ALMOST LIKE ONE LONG UNIVERSITY EDUCATION THAT I NEVER HAD—EVERY DAY I'M LEARNING SOMETHING NEW.

RICHARD BRANSON, FOUNDER OF VIRGIN GROUP

We're going to build our own shipping company." Those probably aren't the wisest words I've ever spoken. After the umpteenth call from an angry customer, though, I could no longer pay the U.S. Postal Service money we didn't have just to get our posters lost in the mail. So, I got creative. A friend of mine—Steve K.—had been helping us for some time and I felt I could trust him with my "big idea" for our new operation: what I now jokingly call our 'ninja shipping system.'

Here's how our ninja shipping worked. We'd charge customers for shipping and handling like normal. Then, we'd pay Steve to play the role of midnight postman. During the day, he'd get on MapQuest (those were the days before everybody had Google Maps in their pocket) and plot out his route as we printed the posters. Once 10 PM hit, Steve would dress in all black, get into his black car, and head out into the night. From dusk to dawn, he'd run up to customers' doors, drop off posters, and then disappear. Dogs and neighbors may have hated us, but ninja shipping was our scrappy way of making things work.

Thankfully, Steve was never shot and our company was never shut down by the federal government. But that was more a matter of luck than skill—not exactly the best inversion when you're trying to build a sustainable business. That was the kind of move you'd expect from a couple of kids with nothing but a good idea and the drive to make it work. No money, no direction, no mentors—we were forced to get creative and see what, if anything, got us from point A to point B. Sometimes, that mix between recklessness and relentlessness leads you to innovate in ways that legitimately change the game. Other times, it takes you straight into the dirt. There will be plenty of time for innovation and success later in this book. For now, this chapter will get you acquainted with the times I crashed and burned, what I learned, and how those early failures shaped the future of my business.

Friends Like These

In chapter 5, I introduced you to MSP designs—the early version of UTP that I started up with a graphic designer friend at Dominican University. After we left college, my friend and I moved in together and started in on the business full-time. On the surface, we were doing great. We were regularly working tournaments and even brought on our first "employee", although she was more like a mother to us and quickly worked her way up to become a part-owner. As good as that all *looked*, not everything was as kosher as it seemed. The business made some money, of course, but my partner and I were having trouble getting by. As it turns out, landlords and grocery stores don't have much sympathy for guys with "irregular cash flow." So, we had our own little survival system. Whenever we took a cash order, we'd divvy it up between us and figure out the overhead later. Not the best way to handle accounting, but it worked.

Something in me knew it was a bad idea to pocket revenue like that, but it wasn't until my partner and our employee called me on it that I realized how bad an idea it was.

I'd recently worked an event with one of my weekend team members. We'd taken a huge order from a Russian team and, like usual, pocketed the cash. No big deal, right? Wrong. When I took that money, I neglected to tell my partner or our employee what I'd done. So, when the team called up the following week to add something to their order, my partner had no idea who he was talking to and why. I'll spare you the gory details, but you can imagine what he thought I was trying to do. He and our employee immediately accused of me stealing from the company. Sparks flew, things got incredibly awkward, and I soon had to walk away from the company altogether.

This was one of the most catastrophic moments in my life. Shortly after the blowup, I went to visit my mother in Texas for a few days. When I came back, I found that my ex-partner had also become my ex-roommate, taking virtually *all* of our furniture with him when he left. I remember walking into that empty apartment (which I could no longer afford on my own), sitting on the floor, and crying. I had hit rock bottom: my bank account was empty, my business was dead, and I barely had a place to lay my head. After 5-10 minutes of sobbing, though, I got up, dusted myself off, walked to the bathroom, and looked in the mirror. Staring at my reflection, I told myself to appreciate this moment at the bottom because I was never coming back. I never have, and I never will.

Andre the Partner

After leaving MSP Designs, I started multiple companies, each with a different partner. For reasons I'll get into below, each of those partnerships fizzled. My last partnership—VanGo Imaging—was a game-changer for me on a number of levels. I'd started it with a poker buddy named Andre whose experience in corporate America made him a real asset to the business. It was with Andre that I first started printing on-site at tournaments in 2010. Before that, I never could figure out the best way to ship posters to customers (see above). Now, though, we could print their posters on-site, frame them up, and hand them off. Thanks in large part to that "innovation," we were able to expand to more than one crew in 2011 and gross our first million dollars in revenue in 2012.

All that success notwithstanding, VanGo was my greatest business lesson yet. Personality-wise, Andre and I were complete opposites. He was a stone-cold realist with a laser-focus on execution. I was an idealistic Midwesterner with a big personality and a deep love for people. For me, entrepreneurship was a means to an end. Money was nice, but I cared more about flexibility, freedom, and lifestyle. I was passionate about the business and put in the blood and sweat to show it, but I also wasn't afraid to put the work down and live my life outside VanGo. After all, what was entrepreneurship all about if I had to live like a slave to my own business? Andre, on the other hand, was all work and no play. He came from corporate America, and his measure of success had a lot more to do with money than mine did.

Long-story short, Andre wanted more out of me than I was willing to give. So, after 4 years of friction, he and I decided to go our separate ways. Andre was my "last" partner, and our split eventually led to the formation of UTP. Before I could get there, though, I had to stop and survey all that my business had been through up to that point. Surely, there had to be some reason why I couldn't keep a partnership together and a company open for more than just a handful of years.

What's Wrong With Me?

I'll never forget what Andre said to me shortly before we split: "the more I get to know you, the less impressed I am by you." Ouch. This guy was more than a partner; he was a friend, and his words cut me to the core. If he were just an acquaintance, I could blow it off. But this guy *knew* me, so I couldn't ignore what he said. There's an old Hebrew proverb that says, "Faithful are the wounds of a friend." Well, Andre wounded me, but it didn't feel all that friendly or faithful—at least, not at the time. 6 years later, though, I'm happy to say we've restored our friendship. In fact, Andre even came on to work at UTP in 2015 and has been with us ever since.

Out of that split, I was forced to take a hard look at myself and my history. In under 10 years, I'd lost 4 partnerships—really, 4 friendships—and closed 4 companies. Thanks to Andre's comment, I couldn't ignore the common denominator in each of those failures: me. But *what* was it about me that led to all those broken businesses? After a lot of soul-searching and deep thought, I realized that the problem wasn't my work ethic or my sales skills. It wasn't because I was bad at building and keeping relationships. In fact, that relational work was (and still is) what I do best.

No, the deep problem underlying my failed partnerships had nothing to do with my professional or interpersonal skills. The problem was my "picker." In choosing partners, I'd always let proximity be my guide. My definition of the "right partner" was whoever happened to be standing in front of me. As long as they had a desire to run a successful business, they were a potential partner. What never entered into my thinking was whether that person shared my values or whether "success" to them looked the same as it did to me. In failing to take the time to understand whether my partners and I synced up at the deep level of vision and values, I set myself up to fail every time. It's as if I met a girl in Vegas, married her on the strip, and then wondered why we didn't end up spending the rest of our lives together.

The deep lesson I learned out of all this wasn't just about finding the "right people," though. It was also about *becoming* the right person. As I've already alluded to in earlier chapters, there's a real sense in which you become the people you choose to surround yourself with. That's why, whenever we hire a new team member, we devote a significant portion of the interview to learning about their friend circle. We're not nosy; we just want to know who this potential hire has allowed to influence their life.

But influence is a two-way street. Before UTP, I loved having people around who looked up to me—people *I* could influence instead of the other way around. I'm not saying all my partners fit that mold. If I have to be honest, though, too many of my decisions in hiring and partnering didn't pay enough attention to what others could bring to enrich me and our business. As a result, I suffered for not having people around who could challenge my perspective and motivate me to think and do better. Today, I've learned to love being the dumbest guy in the room. It's only when I'm with people who stretch me that I can truly learn and grow.

Tell Me Lies, Tell Me Sweet Little Lies

Becoming the person you want to be takes deep, gut-wrenching work. In that season after VanGo broke up, I had to do a lot of introspection, trying to figure out who I was and why I kept running into dead ends. When I did, I didn't just discover my broken "picker." I discovered my broken relationship with reality. When you're young and just getting started in business, you have this intense drive to perform for other people. The last thing you want for them to see is how well you *aren't* doing. So, you put on a show. You tell them things are going great when they really aren't. You boast about your wins, but you don't share your losses. You turn into something like a compulsive liar, not because you deliberately want to mislead people but because you've told *yourself* so many lies that you can no longer tell what's true and false.

That's where I lived for a long time. On a personal level, it put me at odds with partners, friends, and family members. On a practical level, it drove me deep into debt as I used credit cards to run my business and shore up operational losses. $30,000 in the hole later, I had to learn from guys like Dave Ramsey—author of *The Total Money Makeover*—how to get honest about my situation. I had to admit how my business was really doing and make a plan to build it further. I had to get on the phone with my creditors, fess up to my situation, and pledge that I'd pay them back every penny as soon as possible. That was a humbling process, but it taught me what it means to own your failures and learn from them (see chapter 2).

Getting Honest About What You Can and Can't Do

Another challenge in early business isn't just proving yourself to your peers; it's proving yourself to customers. At one of our first events, a mother came up and asked if we would do individual shots. We'd never done anything like that before, but I fired back confidently, "Of course, we do!" So, I went out on the field and took shots of all the kids. I then collected money from the parents and promised to deliver the finished product within a week—pretty reckless, considering we'd never done anything like this before. When it came time to design their posters, though, I realized I had taken every photo from the front when the players only had numbers on the *back* of their jerseys! I had all these photos but no clue which kid was which. I frantically dialed up coaches and asked them to help me identify the kids, but that only got me so far. I must've got a hundred phone calls from angry parents. They'd all paid in advance and, when their posters didn't show up, they figured we must be a scam. It was a complete and utter disaster. Everyone thought we had taken their money and ran!

Look, I'm all for thinking big and leaning into uncertainty—that kind of work will lead you into incredible growth. Stretching yourself, however, is different than bending over backward. I had no business trying to snap those individual shots. I wasn't being honest with my customers or with myself when I told them I could do it. I paid the price for that mistake, but I also learned a valuable lesson that'd seriously influence the way we do things going forward. Today, we've built a system that allows us to provide custom posters for thousands of kids each weekend. We didn't get there by recklessly shooting from the hip every time a new opportunity came our way, but from taking the time to think carefully about whether an idea truly meshed with who we are as a company. If a customer brings us an idea, we listen, take notes, and carefully weigh the pros and cons. Sometimes, we'll even reach out to the customer for additional feedback before we decide whether or not to move forward with the new product.

Through that process, we've gotten crystal clear about what we can and what we can't (really, won't) do. With that added level of intentionality, we've been able to lean into ideas that make sense and away from those that don't. We've also figured out how to tell the difference between a good idea (individual shots) and bad execution (see above). As a result, we've learned from my mistakes and turned individual posters into a huge part of our overall business.

Conclusion: Becoming Who You Are

Why have I shared all this with you? So you can pity me? Absolutely not! This has been a mere fraction of what it looks like to start a business. Too many entrepreneurs step into this world with stars in their eyes, thinking they can just come up with a stellar idea, put it in the field, and watch it take off without any kind of friction. That's just not reality. I can't tell you how thankful I am for that. I would not have the tools and experience to meet the complexity I face on a daily basis if I hadn't failed early on. I wouldn't know what to look for in new hires. I wouldn't know how to think critically about major decisions. I wouldn't know how to keep our team focused on the main things. In sum, I wouldn't be who I am today.

If the failures of my early days were the price I had to pay for the maturity that led us to where we are today, then I'd call that a good deal. You're going to make your own mistakes and pay your own dues, but my hope is that you'll learn something from my story. Tell the truth, watch who you surround yourself with, and don't be too proud to admit it when you discover areas of your life in need of significant improvement. Be honest with yourself and others; that's the only way you'll become tomorrow the person you wish you were today.

Power to Your People

> "THE SINGLE GREATEST 'PEOPLE SKILL' IS A HIGHLY DEVELOPED AND AUTHENTIC INTEREST IN THE OTHER PERSON.
>
> BOB BURG

When my daughter was 9 years old, she came and asked me for $10. Apparently, a friend was starting a business and my little girl wanted to invest. Of course, I gave her the money. I didn't know anything about the kid or the business, but I loved the lesson they were learning. Often, new entrepreneurs struggle with fundraising. They think raising money looks like whatever they see on Shark Tank. As a result, they never get into the gritty reality of scraping together capital. They never learn how to tap their built-in network of friends and family because they don't even consider that to be an option. In the process, they don't just cut themselves off from funding; they miss out on the *human* resources that lie all around them. Business is a team sport, and you won't make it unless you learn how to lean on the people around you for support—financial or otherwise. That's precisely what my daughter and her friend were starting to learn.

In this chapter, we're going to talk about the incredible impact your "people" can have on your business. When I say "people," I mean that network of friends, family, associates, colleagues, and acquaintances that you rub elbows with in the course of your normal life. In my business, these people have spelled the difference between failure and success. Whether they've partnered with me, invested in my company, or come to work for us, the people in my life are responsible for bringing us to where we are today.

In Chapter 7, I shared about the early days of my business and the challenges I faced in choosing the "wrong" people to partner with me. In this chapter, I'm going to revisit the question of partnership to help you think about who might best help *you* build your business. Zooming out, we'll also look at investment and how to invite others to help fund your business. Whether we're talking about partners or investors, this chapter will show you a few practical ways to map out and tap into your network. Before we get to that, though, I need to introduce you to the tool that's helped *me* more than anything else in business—a tool I hope you'll lean on to do the necessary work laid out in the pages to come.

My Killer App: The Yellow Legal Pad

The legal pad was invented in the 19th century by a 24-year-old papermill worker named Thomas Holley. As the story goes, this kid stitched together a bunch of unwanted paper scraps and sold them off as cut-rate notepads. And the company he founded—the American Pad and Paper Company—still exists today! I love that story for two reasons. First, Holley reminds me of myself. He had a "crazy" idea and he made it work. Second, he took leftover scraps and turned them into something valuable, and the pad he invented might honestly be the most valuable tool I've ever owned.

You'll never catch me without a yellow legal pad close by. The pad is where I jot down all my thoughts. When we're facing problems in the business, my go-to move is to sit down with my pad and write everything out. If I'm planning my day, I put it all on the pad. If I'm trying to come up with a strategy, I write it on the pad. Keeping a running tab of action items, problems, and solutions allows me to spy out patterns in my thinking and our operations. When I see those patterns, I can start thinking more holistically about what's going on and what higher-level decisions need to be made.

In this chapter, I'm going to share a couple exercises for getting to know your people. When I do, I'll tell you to grab your legal pad. As much as I swear by my yellow pad of paper, it doesn't matter what that looks like for you. Maybe it's an iPad or a Moleskine. It could be a batch of cocktail napkins for all I care. What matters is that you find a systematic way to record what's going on in your business and your thinking. If you can flesh out and deal with at least one problem per week, you'll end your year with a "book" of 52 problems, complications, decision-points, and solutions. In my business, these ever-developing hierarchies of thinking-on-paper have allowed me to track the big-picture trends in and around our business, anticipate new issues on the horizon, and create structures that avoid the mistakes of our past. Call it low-tech, but the legal pad has been (and continues to be) the most powerful tool I've used to run my business.

Howdy There, Partner

Moving from pads back to people, let's begin by looking again at partnerships. After my 4th partnership fell apart, I decided it'd be best if I went it alone in founding UTP. That's not to say I think partners are a bad idea for everyone. They're just a bad idea *for me*. Some people work best with the collaborative input and operational help of a partner. If that's you, then this section is going to look at a process for choosing the right partner based, in part, on my history of choosing the *wrong* ones, but mostly on my experience in building a team of more than 130 outstanding people.

VIRTUES AND VALUES

To choose the right partner, you've got to begin with virtues and values. To me, the most important thing about a partner isn't necessarily his or her talent, as important as that may be. What I want more than anything in a partner is someone who aligns with me at the core level of virtues and values. More specifically, I'm looking for people who are self-motivated and can fill their own schedule with *productive* activity—not just busywork. I don't care if you're the smoothest salesman or the best graphic designer on the planet; without those characteristics, we're not going to work well together.

What do *you* value? Grab your legal pad and jot down the things you'd want to see in a partner. What words come to mind? Hard-working? Ethical? Generous? Strategically-minded? Write each word down on the left side of your paper and leave a little space so that you can flesh out what you mean. Take it a step further and jot down *why* those values matter to you. Don't rush this. Take all the time you need to reflect on your ideal partner. If you're going to hand this person a significant chunk of the business, then you can't afford to fly through this crucial step.

TECHNICAL SKILLS

Of course, values aren't *everything*. You need people who are actually going to be able to help you *do the work*. Flip your pad to a new page and start anticipating the kinds of operational help you'll need in the future. Are you going to need a bookkeeper? A graphic designer? A business developer? A facilities person? Don't make the mistake of thinking you'll be the one to figure all this stuff out. Instead, anticipate your future needs and start asking yourself what kind of people you'll need to help you fulfill them.

Here's where it pays off to understand yourself first. Take a sheet in your pad to list out your strengths and weaknesses. Where are you strong in the business? What do you love to do? What can you knock out easily? On the flip side, which activities take you the longest and require the most energy from you? What do you hate to do? Where do you lack the experience to serve your company well? In answering these questions, you're looking to develop a clear vision of what you can and can't do for the business. With those things in mind, you can take a look at your anticipated needs and start to think about what kind of partner you'll need to come in and shore up your weak spots.

WHO AND WHAT

Once you've settled on the values and skills you want in a partner, it's time to flip the page and start writing down names. List out *everyone* you know and could reasonably ask to partner with you. From there, you've got a process of elimination on your hands. First, you can strike out everyone on the list you wouldn't trust to go into business with you. Second, scratch off anyone who doesn't line up with your core values. Next, take the names that are left and list out their strengths, weaknesses, passions, and skills as best as you can. Then, start matching people up. Is there anyone on your list who fits with your values, excels in your weak areas, and brings necessary skills to the table? If there is, write their name down on a new sheet of paper. If you've got multiple people like that, develop a prioritized list. Now, it's time to make a few phone calls.

The process I just walked you with is invaluable for choosing a potential partner, but it doesn't just apply to partnership. In spelling out the values and skills you want to see in a partner, you'll also take important steps towards defining what you want to see in pretty much *everyone* who touches the inside of your business. Strategic partners, vendors, team members, contractors, etc.—a smart business owner takes care to ensure all these people align with his or her vision for the company. Trust me, you don't want to hire people that can't (or won't) get on board with your core values.

Putting the Fun Back in Fundraising

For new entrepreneurs, just thinking about fundraising is enough to make them sweat. If you've never been there, it's hard to know where to begin. A few years ago, a mentor completely changed the way I looked at raising money. UTP had a problem: we wanted to expand into new locations but didn't have the capital. So, my mentor had me come up with a plan to get each city profitable, put the numbers together, and pitch it to tournament directors as an investment opportunity. This was a killer idea on two fronts. First, we got the money we needed. Second, we created a competitive advantage because these directors could only earn a return on their investment if we succeeded. This was a huge step in our business and part of the reason why we're in 31 locations today.

The specifics behind my plan probably don't apply to you, but the principle is what really matters. What my mentor showed me was the power of breaking down your business plan into concrete bits that you can then describe and sell to others. I got directors to invest in me because I gave them a very clear idea of what we were doing, what we'd need from them, and what they could expect in return. At the end of that day, whether you're investing in real estate or government bonds, that's how it's supposed to work. You pay X, I do Y, and you get back Z.

Before you go looking for money, take the time to lay out your operation. You need to understand exactly what you need from investors, how you intend to use it, and what you can offer in return. As you do, disabuse yourself of the idea that you're going around looking for handouts. That's not what this is. You're not begging for money. Instead, you're offering an opportunity. You're inviting people to come and be a part of something new and exciting. You're challenging them to take their confidence in your vision and convert it into a better world for you, them, and anyone else who's touched by your business. So, figure out what you have to offer and get excited about going out there to present it. Do that, and you'll find all the help you need—financial or otherwise.

Looking for Cash in All the Right Places

New entrepreneurs often think they need to experience early success before they can start raising money. While that may be true in some contexts, most of the time I've found it to be an excuse based in fear more than anything. The beginning—before you've gotten off the ground—is the *best* time to start raising funds. Let's say you need $2,500 in seed capital for your new company. If you've read the section above and mapped out a plan for a solid idea, you'd be surprised how easy it is to put together a handful of friends and family to pitch in those funds. People today are readier than ever to invest in new startups. They've seen the stories in magazines like Forbes and Inc. about successful new startups. They want to feel like they're getting in on the ground floor of the next Amazon or Apple. You just might be the next Jeff Bezos!

When you *do* get people to commit, remember to always under-promise and over-deliver. Let's say you need that $2,500 I mentioned above. Let's also say you managed to bring in 5 investors at $500 each with a promised return of 20% ($600) in 6 months. As that time goes by, keep your investors in the loop on the business—wins, losses, struggles, triumphs. Never let them feel like you've disappeared with their money. When that 6-month mark hits, do your level best to pay them back $700 instead of the $600 you originally promised. Why? Because there's going to come a day when you need to raise $5,000 instead of $2,500. And who do you think is going to be first in line to jump on that opportunity? Keeping and exceeding your promises is how you build a network of reliable investors—especially when your early investors start connecting you with their friends.

EXERCISE · BUILD YOUR FUNDING NETWORK

For this exercise, I want you to grab your legal pad and make a list like the one you made for partners. This time, you're going to list out potential funding sources. Write down **everyone** you know. Then, write down people **they** know (for example, your best friends' rich uncle). Next, assign a number from 1-10 next to each name. A 1 means you're sure that person **won't** invest in your business. A 10 means you're sure they've got the money and the interest to throw funds your way. Starting

---

with the 5's, reach out to the people on your list (emails, phone calls, lunches, etc.) to see if they'd be interested in investing in your business. As you gauge their interest, change their rating accordingly. Whenever you meet someone new, add their name to the list. This is a great way to build up a roster of investors so that whenever a new opportunity hits and you need funding, you can fire off an email instead of walking down to the bank and applying for a loan.

PRO TIP: The quicker you can develop and solidify a list of qualified and interested investors, the quicker you'll be able to achieve scale.

Even if you don't *need* early investment, the fundraising process is about much more than finding money. Taking the time to distill your business down into a sellable pitch forces you to learn whether you've actually got a viable product on your hand. And asking investors to take a chance on the opportunity you've presented is a lot like early market research. If it only takes you a few meetings to hit your target, then you know you've got something worthy on your hands. If 50 people turn you away, then you know you've got a problem with your business or your pitch—or both. Fundraising is humbling, but if you put yourself out there you'll learn a lot about yourself and your new company. Believe it or not, those lessons are worth *more* than whatever sum of money you're trying to put together.

Conclusion

Back when I was still working at J. Alexander's, one of my regular customers turned up one night with a friend named Peter Foyo. I didn't know Peter or anything about him, but it wasn't long before he and I got to talking about my business. I could tell he was eager to hear more, so we walked out to my car (in the middle of my shift!) so that I could show him a few of my posters and walk him through our process. He was obviously impressed and wanted to know what was keeping me from getting started. The second I mentioned the $4,000 debt on my credit card and the tables I was waiting to clear it up, Peter pulled out his checkbook and wrote me a check for $4,000.

I was floored. What kind of person does something like that? Well, as soon as I was able to get to a computer, I learned exactly what kind of person Peter was. As the former CEO of Nextel Communications Mexico and one of the "heroes" featured in Rhonda Byrne's *The Secret*, Peter was (and has continued to be) an incredibly accomplished businessman. I can't do his story justice here, but he truly came from nothing in order to climb to the top of his field. As I read his story, I was stunned that he would take an interest in me. I absolutely could not waste that connection, so I made it a point to keep in touch while I grew my business. As the years passed, Peter liked what he saw and progressively got more involved until, in 2015, he bought a 10% stake in UTP.

I can't capture in words what Peter has done for our company, but I can tell you that we wouldn't be where we are today if it weren't for him. That's why, inviting someone to partner or invest in your business is worth all the risk that comes with the invitation. I'll admit it; the topics we've covered in this chapter are some of the scariest stuff we'll tackle in this book. Choosing a partner to share in your business is a huge decision.

You're yoking your future to another person and hoping that you've made the right choice. On the investor front, you're throwing yourself out there and asking people to take a chance on you. You're putting up serious relational capital in exchange for investment. That's a bold move, but a necessary one. It'll connect you with the funds you need and, eventually, the investor-partners who can help take your company to the next level. Most importantly, it'll give you the entrepreneurial skills you need to keep pushing your business forward.

You can't let fear stop you. You can't turn away an investor just because you're scared. You can't turn down a partner—assuming they meet your criteria—just because you don't know how the future will turn out or you're worried they'll learn your business and then go start their own. I've known these fears myself. But, in the end, the value that good people will bring to your business far outstrips anything that *might* happen in the future. Business is a team sport. There are people out their like my daughter with a little bit of cash and a whole lot of love who want to help you succeed. Let them.

Good Problems to Have

CHAPTER 09

> "WHETHER YOU THINK YOU CAN, OR
> THINK YOU CAN'T — YOU'RE RIGHT.
>
> HENRY FORD, FOUNDER OF THE FORD MOTOR COMPANY

Back at the beginning of this book, I shared one of the most important lessons I ever learned: you can tell a lot about a business by the quality of its problems. So far, you've read quite a bit about the early problems I faced and some of the crazy ways I tried to solve them. In this chapter, we're going to focus more on the issues we encountered as the business began to mature. These weren't problems that arose out of incompetence or inexperience. Instead, they were the legitimate complications every company has to deal with as it grows and matures. In other words, these were "good" problems because they forced us to innovate our way to the next level. They trained us to be relentless, and to keep moving forward no matter what obstacle stood in our way.

A Real Frame Job

Back when we first started printing on-site, we quickly learned that customers were eager to pay for *framed* posters. Easy enough, right? Not so much. Getting the frames wasn't hard; we just went to Michael's. Transporting them, on the other hand, turned out to be more complicated than we had anticipated. On our very first attempt to tote frames along with us to an event, the "box" we built to carry them failed as soon as we hit the first stoplight, and everything came crashing down on the buddy I'd enlisted to help that weekend. Not a great way to start off our experience with framing.

Thankfully, we soon figured out how to get frames safely to events. For a couple years, that process worked well for us. As I shared back in Chapter 2, though, Michael's let their quality slip and we were left scrambling to find a new supplier. When we couldn't find a good option, we started our own framing company in Texas. 6 hellish months later, we let that company go and found someone else to make our frames. That arrangement worked for a while, but we never could dial in a long-term solution. 3 years into our struggle, I began to realize that we were too dependent on outside suppliers. Our impulse to start our own framing operation was the right one; we just bungled the execution by relying on the wrong people and trying to do it far from home. So, what did we do? We decided to build our own framing facility.

It was 2015 and we had just moved into our office in Rockdale, so we had the space and resources to build our operation the way *we* wanted. In case you didn't know, you can't exactly Google how to build a framing facility. So, we figured it out the best we could. We built tables with wheels on them so we could frame during the week and roll everything out of the way to make space for our design team on the weekends. We rigged our miter saws to deal with the 10-foot long pieces of MDF molding we used to make the frames. We covered everything in vinyl to keep the wood from getting scratched. We fashioned jigs and stoppers to make it all as streamlined as possible. We even bought a 10x20 canopy and decked our guys out with gas masks and goggles just to deal with all the sawdust. It was a slick operation, and we were cranking out frames for less than we'd ever paid in the past.

The trouble was, our operation was an accident waiting to happen. When I brought in Jim Stemper—a friend in the framing business who eventually came on to run one of our independent locations—to take a look at our facility, his jaw hit the floor. Right away, he said, "Dude, you can get arrested on so many violations from OSHA right now!" As far as Jim was concerned, our place was a death trap. Still, we were getting high-quality frames built at volume. I don't want to say he was impressed, but he was definitely surprised at what we were able to accomplish with nothing more than our own ingenuity and relentless drive. After Jim picked his jaw up off the floor, he walked us through the process and helped us find the equipment we needed to do the job right.

About as soon as we perfected our framing operation, we decided to shut it down. Why? As all this was going on, I found out that my old partner Andre had been trying to reach me. He had realized a lot after our split and wanted to work together again. When he joined UTP, he didn't just bring in a bunch of new contacts from his previous business; he also brought us a new frame supplier. At that point in our life, we were in a much better position to work with a supplier. In building frames, we learned a great deal about *consuming* them, which put us in a much better position to understand the business and strike a solid deal with our new supplier. Today, I'm happy to say we've got a steady stream of high-quality frames rolling in at a price everybody loves.

Growing up is Hard to Do

In my line of work, scale is a complicated beast. We do plenty of business online (more on that later), but our model is built around what happens on-site at tournaments. At a high level, the equation is pretty simple: more sites = more revenue. We added our first expansion site in 2011. As of this writing in 2019, we've got over 30 locations spread out across the U.S. How we got from there to here is a complicated story and another example of how we had to solve problems one-by-one and innovate as we went along.

Early on, we leaned on tournament directors to drive our expansion. We gave them a setup and provided all the staffing, supplies, and design support they needed to produce and sell posters. We each covered our own expenses and then split the revenue. As simple as that plan seemed, it didn't take us long to figure out that tournament directors make their money running tournaments—not selling posters. As a result, they couldn't put in the time and energy it takes to succeed on site. I don't blame them; these were solid guys that I continue to respect and rely on to this day. They just weren't set up to give our well-oiled machine the inputs it needed to crank out consistent revenue.

After we scrapped the director-model, we decided to try out "franchising." I put franchising in quotes because I'm still not sure to this day whether, legally speaking, what we created might better be called "independent locations." Like the director model, we provided each of our "franchisees" with branding, supplies, and design support. In pretty short order, we added 15 new locations and thought to ourselves, "This is it!" Well, it wasn't. Leaving aside that pesky lawsuit I mentioned in Chapter 1, it just didn't work for us evaporate all our margin trying to get franchisees paid. More importantly, though, we found that the franchise model sacrificed too much in terms of quality control and customer service. At the end of the day, we couldn't maintain the control we needed to ensure that the UTP brand was being represented in the way we wanted it.

In the end, franchises were an expensive distraction. Instead of serving parents and players, I found myself spending more time trying to keep our location owners happy. In dealing with all that complexity, though, the franchising debacle forced us to get serious about expanding on our own terms. As a result, we've turned to hiring out our own locations, paying our local directors a salary plus commission. We give them the training and resources they need to run their own operation and then get out of the way. Still, we hold them close enough to ensure the UTP system continues to operate as it should. This is the model that's allowed us to grow to over 30 locations so far.

From Joliet to Mexico: Migrating Our Graphic Design

Aside from everything that happens on-site (setting up our spot, serving customers, snapping photos, etc.), graphic design has always been one of the most "labor intensive" aspects of our operation. Back in 2014, it became clear to me that we couldn't scale much further unless we put serious thought into developing a dedicated graphic design team. Me, a laptop, and a can of Red Bull just weren't going to work at scale. At first, we hired some college students but immediately ran into issues with attitude. So, instead of hiring older designers who thought they knew it all, we decided to bring in high school kids and train them from the ground up. To find the kids, I went down to Joliet West High School and talked to their graphic design teacher about giving a presentation and inviting some of his students to work for me. He said yes and, long-story short, I found myself interviewing 30 kids, one-by-one, in a little glass meeting room at the Joliet Public Library. By the end of it, I had 10 designers ready to go.

At that time, I was running our "design shop" out of my garage. Professional, I know. When the kids' parents dropped them off for their first day of training, most of them decided to stick around to see whether I was on the up and up. They were skeptical at first, but they slowly realized that this was a legitimate business and I was teaching their kids important skills. That entire process was a surreal experience for me. It was during this time that I learned just how much I love mentoring high school students. Working alongside them, I gained a real insight into how they felt about school, their classes, and college. I got to hear what they were thinking about major life decisions and speak into some of the most important issues they were facing. They were an amazing group of people with great hearts, and I was grateful to play a role in shaping their lives.

The relationships I developed with those kids and their parents continue to this day. Still, the high school experiment was never meant to last. Eventually, we moved out of my garage and into a 3,000 square-foot warehouse in Rockdale, where the team swelled to nearly 30 designers. At that point, I could only spend so much time with each individual student. I'm sorry to say that, in that lower-accountability environment, we ended up paying a lot of people to watch Netflix (a serious problem facing companies today). On the strength of the relationships we'd built, I could address some of these instances but not all. It was difficult, but we decided this wasn't going to work long-term. With graduation on the horizon and many of our designers preparing to go off to college, we wrapped up our high school design team and went another way.

Before I was ready to call it quits with the high school kids, Peter Foyo hit me with an idea I'd never considered: outsourcing. At first, I hated the idea of swapping out the kids for a bunch of people in another country. But I trust Peter completely, so when it came time to close our high school operation, I gladly connected with one of his guys in the Dominican Republic. After a quick chat on the phone, I found myself online booking tickets to bring a few guys up to the U.S. for a meet and greet *the next day*. Of course, they didn't speak English, so I had to scramble for an interpreter. Thankfully, one of the kids we hired from Joliet West who has since become one of our most valuable team members—Erica—grew up in Mexico and was able to help me out. So, we brought these guys in, had a great conversation, and began to set up shop in the DR.

Everything was great at first. We trained the guys who would run our design center so that they could turn around and train up their team. Through the first half of 2017, everything hummed along smoothly. When the summer rolled around, the entire business picked up the pace and we had to triple the design team. For these guys, that was no sweat. They were glad to grow their side of the operation. But then Summer ended. It was time to ratchet back down our graphic design budget and shrink our team and our budget back down to size. One problem: our guys in the DR weren't having it.

The guys we had hired to run our office were smart; they knew I'd shut down our design operation in the U.S. and that we were dependent upon them to get our posters done. They had all the leverage. At least, that's what they thought. Right away, I got on the phone with Erica explained the situation. Then, I asked her, "Do you have any family in Mexico who'd be interested in working for us?" She told me about her cousin who might be interested, but that he had a good job and wouldn't want to risk it. I was in a tough spot, so I told her I'd double his pay and send his first check *that afternoon*. Sure enough, I sent the check, he quit his job, and the next day

Erica and Julie were on a plane headed down to Mexico to fire up our new design office. When I got off the phone, I reached out to our guys in the DR: "Thanks, but no thanks. We're done."

In Mexico, we used the exact same approach we used at Joliet West, except we went into a local university instead of a high school. That first day, we recruited 10 people. Within a week, we had them trained, set up in an office close to the university, and ready to go. They were a little slow to begin with, but thanks to our efficiency, we were able to double the size of the team to compensate. We hired a manager to run it all and serve as our main point of contact. We built in plenty of redundancy, eventually setting up a second office in another town with a completely different staff. We even had each of the offices hooked up with different internet service providers. Why? Because we were never going to put ourselves in a position where a single person could take our company hostage ever again. And we weren't about to rest our entire design on the back of only *one* utility provider in Mexico.

To this day, our design operation runs like a well-oiled machine. We've got just under 40 designers working for us, with 90 or so on the waiting list. Our design costs are fixed at a great rate, which helps us quite a bit with budgeting. We pay our designers a fantastic wage and hook them up with skills that will benefit them long after they leave. But, first and foremost, we focus on creating an environment where they won't want to leave. In an environment where you're paid well and are taken care of by people who genuinely care about your well-being, there's not a lot of incentive to leave. And, with 90 people looking over your shoulder and waiting to take your chair, there's plenty of incentive to show up on time and get the job done. When that happens, everybody wins.

Conclusion

When I started in this business, the problems I faced and the questions I asked were important, but they were basic:

- How do I start a business?
- How do I even sell a poster?
- How do I find customers?
- How do I find and get into events?
- How do I ship posters?

Today, the problems have matured, and the questions I'm asking reflect a far more complex business environment than I ever could've imagined when I first got started:

- How do you keep vendors and suppliers from holding you hostage?
- How do you quarterback a nationwide network of salespeople?
- How do you develop and manage multiple products?
- How do you scale a marketing effort in multiple cities?
- How do you negotiate with workers in other countries?
- How do translate between different languages and cultures?
- How do you transfer money to different countries without ticking off the IRS?

These questions reflect 15 years of hard work and growth. For every problem we've solved, a new and more complex set of problems eventually cropped up. For every question we answered, a nest of follow-ups sprang right up. Such is life in the business world. The only way you grow—as a person and as a company—is by facing these problems head on and innovating your way forward. The one thing that kept us going, whether it was in the face of supply chain woes, growing pains, or design troubles, was our relentless commitment to excellence. We weren't going to quit. And we refused to compromise when it came to building a place where team members could be valued, customers taken care of, and revenue maintained at a sustainable level.

If I've learned anything from the stories I shared above, it's this: every problem has a solution if you'll just keep working at it. What problems are you facing today? What questions are you asking? Grab your legal pad. Get them out of your head and down onto paper. Start brainstorming solutions. You don't have to solve everything right away. Just figure out the next step, then take it. Keep moving forward. You'll make mistakes—sometimes huge ones. But, step by step, you *will* innovate your way forward as long as you just keep moving. The problems you face tomorrow will look nothing like what you're dealing with today. That's a good thing. They'll be better problems. They'll stretch you and challenge you to grow in ways you never anticipated. Embrace the challenge and stay relentless. That's the only way forward in business and in life.

From Good Problems to Great Work

CHAPTER 10

> "I'M CONVINCED THAT ABOUT HALF OF WHAT SEPARATES THE SUCCESSFUL ENTREPRENEURS FROM THE NON-SUCCESSFUL ONES IS PURE PERSEVERANCE.
>
> STEVE JOBS

You can't learn how to build a business by just sitting around in your armchair and dreaming about success. You've got to get out there, bump up against real tension, and learn to innovate your way forward. Over the course of 15 years, I've faced my fair share of tension. You read about some of it in Chapter 9. There's no getting around it: business problems hurt. They threaten our sense of safety and demand resources—time, money, focus, energy—that we'd rather spend elsewhere. Still, problems are how we level up our entrepreneurial game. No problems, no growth.

In this chapter, I want to help *you* get ready for the problems you'll inevitably face as you set off to build your business. More than that, I want to show you how you can leverage those problems into better work for you and your company. Ready? Grab your pad and let's get started.

Become a Prophet for Profit

To be honest, I hate it when people use clichés like "expect the unexpected." Still, there's truth in that pithy little bit of nonsense. In my business, I've come to discover that one of the most beneficial things an entrepreneur can do is learn how to anticipate future problems and map out their solutions in advance. Here's an example of what that might look like:

BUMPING UP WEBSITE TRAFFIC

Imagine I've got my own ecommerce business. I want more traffic to my site, so I'm going to start marketing on Facebook. For now, I'll budget $50 a day for ads.

What could go wrong? Here's what:

1. I don't get charged and my ads don't show up. [No Show]
2. The ads show, I spend my full $50, but nobody clicks the ad. [No Love]
3. People click the ad, but nobody buys anything. [No Dice]

These are live outcomes—they happen all the time in social media marketing. Acknowledging that, I need to think about what I'll do if I encounter them.

Here's my initial contingency plan:

1. No Show
   a. Double-check to see if I've set my ads up correctly.
   b. Re-evaluate my demographics.
   c. Broaden my target audience to get more ad appearances.
2. No Love
   a. Double-check my target to make sure I'm hitting the right people.
   b. Redesign/rewrite my ad for more engagement.
   c. Run an A/B test between the old and new ads.

3. No Dice
   a. Double-check my target.
   b. Make sure my ad's landing page is optimized for conversion.
   c. Rewrite my landing page; A/B test the old and new versions.

What I just laid out for you is a bare-bones decision tree: if *a* happens, then I'll do *b*; if *c* happens, then I'll do *d*. Early on, your thought process will look very much like this simple example. As you mature in business, though, things will get much more complicated. The decision tree I shared above could easily go 3 more levels deep, depending on how complex my marketing campaign is and how committed I am to making this specific campaign work. In the beginning, you can only anticipate so much. As you gain experience, though, you'll learn more about what *could* go wrong from times when things actually *do* go wrong. Until then, train up your prophetic powers by reading books (like this one!) and blogs, listening to experts, and learning from other people's experience.

Contingency plans like these are about more than strategy. The simple act of anticipating problems, formulating solutions, and getting it all out on paper won't *just* leave you with a handy action plan when you face trouble. It'll mature you as a thinker. It'll develop a habit (more on those below) of careful anticipation that enables you to think more strategically about every decision you make. Before you know it, you'll be solving problems before they even happen. If you've ever met those incredible people in business who seem to be 6 steps ahead of the game at all times, *this* is how they got there. They weren't born that way; they developed the habit of foresight over years of anticipating and facing down problems in their own lives and businesses. To use the cliché one last time, they've trained themselves to "expect the unexpected." So can you.

Take a Step Back

In his instant classic, *The E Myth*, Michael Gerber wrote about the difference between working "on" vs. "in" your business. The idea is this: you may be the best baker in your city, but that has nothing to do with how well you can *run a bakery*. What happens in cases like these is the business owner defaults to what she knows—making cupcakes—and punts on everything else. As a result, she spends all her time working "in" the business instead of working "on" it. I don't care how transcendent your cupcakes are; nobody's going to buy them if you don't know the basics of leasing space, buying equipment, marketing, and everything else that goes into running a business.

When problems arise in your business, your first instinct will be to roll up your sleeves, get *in* there, and do the grunt work. Why? Because you know much more about how to "bake a cupcake" than how to fix a broken supply chain. When you're starting up and you're still small, there's no way around this. Still, don't let that become a trap. No matter how small you are, you have to intentionally step back and look at your problems from the outside—work "on" the business vs. "in" it. Do you notice patterns? Is there a bigger problem that lies behind and beneath your small problems? Is there a person you can hire or a process you can create in order to head these things off at the pass? If you train yourself to ask these higher level questions from the beginning, you'll set yourself up to be a better leader when the time comes to hire more people.

Focus on Meaningful Action

Especially in corporate America, people tend to wear their busyness like a badge of honor. They boast about the 80-hour week they just put in and gloat about the fact that they only slept 4 hours last night. Startups are the worst at this. Often motivated by a sense of false urgency, they grind their team members down to the bone with meaningless work that does *nothing* to contribute to the company's success. Sometimes, all that busywork comes out of the mistaken idea that activity equals productivity. Most of the time, though, it comes out of fear.

Busywork is a great way to avoid the *real* issues that lie in front of you. 6 hours tweaking your site design, for example, is a lot less stressful than having to pick up the phone and explain to a customer why you botched their order. 10 hours rearranging your storeroom is hard work, but not nearly as hard as having to figure out why *your storeroom is full of products that you haven't sold.* Examples like these go to show that busywork isn't just a waste of productive time; it's actually *counterproductive.*

Even if you aren't using busywork to avoid a pressing issue, think of all the more valuable things you could be doing besides simply filling out your schedule with pointless activity: reading good books, developing new business relationships, taking a nap. I'm not kidding about that last one; grabbing a few extras Zs so that you can have more energy and focus for the work that matters is an infinitely better use of your time than spinning your wheels on work that doesn't.

EXERCISE · MAKE A LIST

Some people prefer not to use to-do lists, but I swear by them for three reasons. First, the most obvious benefit of a good to-do list is that it'll help you keep track of everything so that nothing slips through the cracks. Second, the action of checking items off your list can actually encourage you to keep moving forward. Third, to-do lists provide a simple record of your activity so that you can see whether or not the work you're doing is actually meaningful.

If you don't already have one, start keeping a to-do list. I like to use an app called Wunderlist, but there are plenty of high-tech (apps) and low-tech (legal pad) options out there. For the first week, put **everything** on your list. On Saturday night, sit down and look at what you've accomplished. On a scale of 1 to 5, make a note by each action showing whether the action was crucial to your success (5) or busywork (1). What patterns do you see? What do you need to avoid next week? What do you need to pursue?

Deep Values + Quality Habits = Life and Business Success

In his bestselling book, *Atomic Habits,* James Clear shows how the littlest changes we make in our lives are responsible for the most significant results we see in the long-term. "If you want to predict where you'll end up in life," Clear says, "all you have to do is follow the curve of tiny gains or tiny losses, and see how your daily choices will compound ten or twenty years down the line."[3] You don't become a good father by just showing up and cheering at your kid's championship game. No, you become the father you want to be in the 1,001 mundane little things that happen between the moment your kid signs up for little league and the day the season ends: the late afternoon drive to practice, the hundredth load of laundry, the heart-to-heart chat after a hard loss.

In the same way, you don't just wake up a successful entrepreneur. You make a million little decisions—all the way from bringing on a new equity partner to holding the door open for your administrative assistant—

---

[3] Atomic Habits, 18.

that either lead you *toward* or *away from* your ultimate vision of success. These daily choices aren't so much a product of conscious decision as they are *habits*—"behavior that has been repeated enough times to become automatic."[4] The payoff? Create your habits, and they'll create your life.

The habits I've developed over the years have been essential to my success in business. We can group them up into what I call the 4 E's:

- **Environment** - When it comes to the workplace, surroundings matter more than you think. I always try to do things that create a place where people can feel safe, welcome, and free to be creative.
- **Ethic** - 15-hour days, sleeping in my car or on a couch—these are just a few of the "dues" I've paid over the years. I wouldn't have done those things if I didn't have a strong work ethic driving me forward.
- **Efficiency** - Virtually everything you do can be improved upon in some way. The key to developing a lean system and a productive life is to constantly look for ways to cut down on meaningless repetition.
- **Engagement** - Because growth is always on the other side of tension, you can never be too afraid to engage the hard parts of business— especially when they involve other people. Your success in life will be determined by the number of uncomfortable conversations you're willing to have.

Another helpful way to think about the E's is in terms of *values*. Because I value environment, I pay attention to our workplace and the people in it. Because I'm driven by my small-town work ethic, I expect a lot out of myself and others. Because I'm all about efficiency, I take a fine-toothed comb to *everything* we do. And because I know the value of

---

[4] Ibid., 44.

engagement, I make it a point to never shy away from the tough stuff.

EXERCISE • WRITE OUT YOUR VALUES

What are your values? How do your habits confirm or deny what you say you value? For example, you can't say you **truly** value your office environment if you're a jerk to your team members. Grab your pad and list the values you hold dear in the margins. Leave a couple lines between each. Then, think about your daily habits and list out the different ways in which you either display or betray those values. Take it a step forward and ask what needs to change.

Call in the Robots

Above, I mentioned efficiency as one of the core values that's driven my success in business. Here, I want to expand on that by touching on one of the hottest topics in business today: automation. Simply defined, automation is about rooting out the repetitive processes in your business and assigning them to technology. That way, you can significantly amp up production while freeing your people up to do what only *people* can do: creative work, development, relationship-building, etc.. The other benefit of automation is *consistency*. Computer error pales in comparison to human error, so an automated process virtually guarantees you'll get things right each and every time.

Automation has been crucial in our business. Not too long ago, we started selling custom socks. At first, we had a designer manually place the player's number and last name on the back of a sock. The trouble was, we had trouble with constant misspellings. So, we built out a section of our website where parents could input their kids' names and numbers. Then, the site would work its magic and out would come perfectly proofed, errorless socks. It cost us $7,500 to do, but the money we saved in botched socks and time spent drilling our designers on quality control dwarfed that initial investment.

EXERCISE • AUTOMATE YOUR TO-DO LIST

Grab your to-do list from above. Take a look at all the 1's and 2's on your list. How many of those actions can be bundled up and passed off to an app or a virtual assistant? Platforms like Upwork and Fiverr can put you in touch with a freelancer to do virtually anything you don't want or need to do in your business.

Here is a short list of just 7 things you can start automating today:

1. Contact form follow-ups from your website.
2. Lead nurturing.
3. Birthday greetings.
4. Thank-you notes.
5. Client/customer satisfaction surveys.
6. Booking appointments and setting reminders.
7. Social media marketing.

Conclusion

As I said in the last chapter, I'm grateful for the hurdles I had to jump to get me where I am in business today. A friend and mentor once stressed to me that I'm in the prime of my life as a husband, father, and entrepreneur. Every day I get to work on something I love beside people

I truly enjoy. I'm "in the zone," and the hurdles I face every day are right here in the zone with me. To avoid them would be to run outside my lane and drop out of the race. That's not an option. Instead, I need to run the race and give thanks for the hurdles. The higher they are and the better I clear them, the less likely it is some dark horse will show up and beat me to the finish line.

How about you? Are you ready to run your race? What kind of hurdles lie in your path? What will you do when you get to them? Will you take the time to grab a video recorder and check out your form between laps? Will you get ruthlessly efficient, making sure every stride counts and refusing to take a single step that doesn't? Problems are going to come your way, but if you think carefully about them on the front end and move *toward* them as they occur, they will be incredible catalysts for your growth in life and business. So, embrace the problems, leverage your solutions into quality habits and patterns of work. Always be on the look-out for ways to automate your business, and never let busywork trick you into thinking you've done *real* work. That's how you'll take good problems and turn them into great work for you and your business.

In Ron We Trust

" SO OFTEN PEOPLE ARE WORKING HARD
AT THE WRONG THING. WORKING ON
THE RIGHT THING IS PROBABLY MORE
IMPORTANT THAN WORKING HARD.

CATERINA FAKE, CO-FOUNDER OF FLICKR

Here's what you need to do." That phrase can make or break your life and business. On the backside of those 6 little words, you might get the best advice you've ever heard or the worst. Without a crystal ball, there's no telling which way it'll go. The question is: will you take the advice or leave it? Of course, it makes all the difference in the world *who's* offering their advice. If I'm chatting with a guy on the train and he tells me what to do, then I might entertain him for the sake of conversation, but drop it later that day. But if it's Peter Foyo, I'm all ears.

Figuring out when to take advice and when to ignore it is one of the most important skills you can develop in life and business. As you grow your company, though, there's going to come a time when you can't afford to stop and weigh all the options every time a recommendation hits your inbox. You're going to need to trust the person on the other side of that email and throw your weight behind whatever he or she thinks is best. Without that level of trust, you may be able to surround yourself with a team that gets the job done, but you'll end up running yourself ragged as you try to micromanage every last detail.

Send Me Someone I Can Trust

Back in Chapter 9, I told you all about the graphic design shop we set up in the Dominican Republic and how our designers tried to hold us hostage. Well, before that happened, we decided to use the same guys to build our entire website. They talked a big game about custom design and coding, but what we ended up with was a sloth of a website made up of cobbled-together WordPress plugins. It was slow and heavy. Customers could barely use it and Google wanted nothing to do with it as far as search engine ranking goes. Not exactly a winning formula for doing business online.

You could say I was disappointed, but I wasn't exactly surprised. I got what I paid for. These guys were great when they stayed in their lane and designed posters—not so much when it came to designing web pages. So, I decided I wouldn't make that mistake again. I went on Upwork—one of the major freelancing sites right now—to look for a top-notch web developer. When I found the right guy, I was shocked to learn the prognosis was much worse than I had expected. I thought I needed someone to "fix" my site. What I really needed was someone to scrap the site and build a completely new one.

"Here's what you need to do," my new developer said. But was I going to do it? Was I going to trust the professional I'd hired to give it to me straight? After thinking it through, I decided to take his advice and start from scratch. It was a huge project, so we approached it in phases. I did all the design work myself while our developer handled the code. 18 months and $100,000 later, our site was light-years beyond what we'd started with. It soon became the perfect digital extension of our physical operation, taking what used to be a 3-day revenue window each week and opening it up to 7. The future of retail is a hybrid model like this one—where on-line presence supports off-line sales and vice versa. It feels good to be on the cutting edge. More importantly, we're ready to meet whatever challenges an evolving marketplace may decide to throw our way.

For a business our size, $100,000 was a lot to spend on a web site, but I have no doubt it was worth every penny. I'll tell you a bit more about what our site's done for us below. Suffice it to say that, without this one developer's work, we would not be where we are today. If I hadn't done my homework and forked over the cash to hire a professional I could trust, we would've limped along with a second-rate website. To this day, he continues to do crucial work for us. Remember the sock automation I mentioned in the last chapter? That was all him. Have you guessed his name yet? It's Ron.

Lining and Strengthening Our Bench

After Ron finished building our website, I had a bunch of t-shirts made up that say "In Ron We Trust" on the front. That's what I think about the value Ron personally brought to our business. But, more than that, those four words reflect a deep lesson we learned about how we value potential members of our team. Before Ron, I let my desire for efficiency throttle how much I was willing to lay out for genuine expertise. Whatever money I saved, though, I ended up paying back tenfold in the form of lost revenue and ongoing technical support. It was only when we put value before cost that we freed ourselves to find someone like Ron—a genuine game-changer for our business. Once we learned that lesson, we amped up our human resources budget and started going after people we could barely afford. And can you guess what they did? They found ways to generate value that far outstripped whatever we paid to bring them on board.

I wish I had learned earlier on just how important it is to invest in the players that line your bench. That begins with bringing the right people onto the team. What did that look like for me? I adopted what I call a two-profile system. Profile #1 would describe the position I'm looking to fill and everything that job would require—skills, experience, strengths, passion, etc. Profile #2 would focus on the person—who *they'd* need to be to not just fit that position but to fit into our team as well. In my experience, I've found that as soon as I develop those two profiles, the right person seems to just show up at my door. Set your attention on the things you need, and they'll happen.

But I'm not just talking about hiring the right people and paying them what they're worth. I'm talking about investing in the people you've already got and making them worth more, as well. When I look at the people on our team—whether they're just coming on or they've been with us for years—I try to look at more than just what they have to offer us *today*. I also look at what they have to offer us *tomorrow*. What are the latent skills they bring to the job that may not help us right now but can help us as we develop new lines of business down the road? How can I encourage them to find creative ways to apply their talent to the job? In all, I want to help these people flourish as much as I possibly can. In return, I not only get a "better" worker; I get the joy of watching someone I care about grow to become a better version of him- or herself.

Building People and Platforms for Future Growth

Ron built us a heck of a website. I'm legitimately proud of our online business and am looking forward to growing it even further. But our site isn't just a place to sell products; it's our entire digital infrastructure. We use our site's backend to manage all of our people from all over the world. Through it, we've created a tremendous workflow that keeps our on-site teams in sync with "home-base" and enables us to work seamlessly with our people in Mexico and Indonesia. As we work to expand our on-site teams across the U.S. and into Canada, this technological infrastructure will be key in maintaining the efficiency and consistency that UTP prides itself on. I trust the system to serve us well in the future because I trust the Ron who built it for us.

It's not always easy to trust the people you work with. I've found that, especially when working with people outside the United States, cultural and linguistic barriers make it difficult to establish a solid working relationship. You already saw what happened with our team in the Dominican Republic. Out of that disaster, though, I learned a lot about covering my bases, building in protections, and figuring out who to trust and how far to trust them. As I was writing this book, we had the opportunity to set up a new partnership with a team in Indonesia. The process wasn't easy—I found myself scrambling to set up a 3-way phone call with translator at midnight—but I knew what to expect and how to navigate the situation. Without that background experience, I'm not confident we could have pulled it all together.

Even as we push out our operation into the world, we've learned to strategically *pull in* people when it makes sense. We used to train the staff for our new locations on site. What we've found, though, is that bringing everyone to us is a much more efficient use of our time for training. When they come in, we get the chance to more intentionally educate them on where we've been and where we're going. We give them a clear sense of the potential that lies in front of us and invite them to own their role in helping UTP's future growth.

The entire process creates a more consistent training product and a sense of connection between us and our remote team members. We foster that connection through regular video chats and a dedicated Slack channel. We even encourage healthy competition by publishing weekly sales numbers. We push each other to be better, and we have fun while we do it. This is how you cement a team together. It's also how you cultivate a group of people you can trust to tell you the truth and to go out and get the job done on your behalf.

Conclusion: Entering into the Next Phase

There's much more on the horizon for UTP than what I can share here. We're continuing to develop relationships with tournament directors, add new locations, and expand our product line. The people in our orbit are growing more and more excited to see where we're headed. As I write this, the ink is barely dry on a deal for one of our tournament directors and a long-time friend to buy into the company as an investor. From his perspective as a director, he's seen the value we have to offer, and he knows where we're headed. Even better, his connections to the baseball world almost guarantee that we're going to add quite a few new tournaments to our schedule in the near future.

We couldn't have gotten this far without trust. A whole lot of people have trusted me to deliver on the vision I cast for UTP. And I've trusted on them to help me get us where we're going. Have we arrived? Not by a long-shot. This book isn't a victory lap; it's an invitation to come and see what life *really* looks like when you're an entrepreneur. I've faced my share of problems, and I've seen people at their absolute worst. But one of the most important things I've learned along the way is this: you can't build a business by yourself. You're going to have to trust people to help you. There's no way around that. The trick is finding the people you can trust and setting them free to do their best work. In the next chapter, we'll talk about how to do just that.

CHAPTER 12

How to Build Your Dream Team

> " NETWORKING IS A LOT LIKE NUTRITION
> AND FITNESS: WE KNOW WHAT TO DO, THE
> HARD PART IS MAKING IT A TOP PRIORITY.
>
> HERMINIA IBERRA

During the 1988 Olympics, the United States Men's Basketball team was forced to settle for the bronze after a humiliating loss to the Soviet Union. Coming off 40 years of Cold War tension, the defeat rocked the entire country. So, when the International Basketball Federation (FIBA) voted in 1989 to allow professionals to compete in the Olympic games, the U.S. wasted no time. Coach Chuck Daly and his crew put together the strongest bench ever assembled: Michael Jordan; Magic Johnson; Larry Bird; Charles Barkley; Karl Malone; John Stockton; Patrick Ewing; David Robinson; Clyde Drexler; Scottie Pippen; Chris Mullin; Christian Laettner. When it came time for the 1992 games, the "Dream Team" dominated the court, scoring more than 100 points per game and beating their opponents by an average of more than 40 points.

When I think about the Dream Team, the thing that impresses me most isn't the sheer amount of talent coming off that one bench. No, what really gets me is how the team's coaches were able to mesh the larger-than-life personality that each player brought with him. How do you get Michael Jordan and Magic Johnson to play nice with one another? How do choose whether to start Larry Bird or Patrick Ewing? As the saying goes, it takes teamwork to make the dream work. It wasn't enough for the team to be full of talented *individuals*. They had to work *together* if they wanted to win.

Business is the same. You can have a team full of all-stars. But, if they can't play together, you won't win the game. It doesn't matter how much raw talent you've got on that bench; you need to put your players out on the court and get them to *work together* to execute your game-winning strategy. That's what this chapter is about: finding the *right* people to join your team, coming up with a strategy to use them well, and inspiring everyone to give it their all. By the end of this chapter, you'll have the conceptual and practical tools you need to start building out a team that will help you win in business.

When to Start Building Your Team

One of the trickiest questions for an entrepreneur to navigate is when to hire. A common mistake I see new business owners make is to start hiring too soon. I call it a mistake for a couple reasons. First, when you hire early, you write a check you better be able to cash week in and week out. When you're just starting out and revenue is dicey, that might back you into an uncomfortable corner. Trust me, you don't want to find yourself in a position where you can't afford to pay your people.

Of course, you can get around this problem by raising enough money to fund your payroll. But I still think it's a bad idea to hire early. Why? When you're in the early stages of your business, you're in the trenches. It's on you to make the business work, which means you've got to do pretty much everything. For one thing, that'll teach you humility. More importantly, though, it'll personally acquaint you with the contours of each individual position. When the time finally does come to hire someone to take over that work, you'll have a much better sense of who and what you need, along with a deeper appreciation for the value they bring to the company. You'd never get that if you grabbed a bunch of venture capital and staffed up your entire operation from Day One.

Long story short, you should wait as long as possible before you start hiring people. Unlike basketball, you can get by with a team of one for a while. Be careful, though. There is such a thing as waiting *too* long. When you find yourself working 60 hours a week and banging your head against the wall to do what a professional could handle in minutes, then it's time to hire. Start with limited engagements, farming out tasks to friends you know or freelancers you find online. As you do, look at what your outsourcing and see what can be bundled. If you've got 30+ hours of work you can put together each week, it's time to start thinking about a full-time hire.

Profile the Position, Position the Profile

In the previous chapter, I told you about the two-profile system I use to develop new positions in our company and envision the exact person I want to fill those positions. Here, I want to share a version of that system with you.[5] Grab your legal pad and draw a line down the center. Over the

---

[5] At your current stage, this may not be applicable to you. If not, dog-ear this page, skip this section, and come back to it later when you're ready to start hiring.

left column, write "Position." Over the right, write "Profile." Down the left-hand margin, space out these words: Who, What, When, Where, Why, How. On the left column, answer each of these questions:

- **Who** are you looking for? [Job Title]
- **What** are you hiring them to do? [Job Description and Expectations]
- **When** do you need them? [Hire Date *and* Projected Scheduling Expectations]
- **Where** will they slot into the company? [Organizational Chart]
- **Why** does this position need to exist? [The Problems They'll Solve]
- **How** will they help your company grow? [The Value They'll Bring]

Now, on the right side of the paper, answer these questions:

- **Who** does this person need to be? [Personality & Values]
- **What** kind of experience should they have? [Resume, Qualifications]
- **When** are they willing to work? [Eagerness, Commitment, Scheduling]
- **Where** will they work—local or remote? [Location, Pool of Potential Hires]
- **Why** would they be excited to work here? [Engagement Level]
- **How** will they feel about your business as it stands? [Eagerness to Add Value]

Both sets of questions straddle the fence between quantitative logistics and qualitative vision-casting. That's intentional. As you develop a new position, you'll have to think concretely about what you need, what you're willing to pay, and so on. At the same time, you'll need to think abstractly about the *kind* of person you want to fill the position—who are they, what do they value, how excited are they about getting into the company and helping you solve *your* problems, and so on. By bringing together these two poles of thinking, you'll better position yourself to make the best possible hire.

As you work on this exercise, you'll probably end up scribbling all over your page and spilling out into others. You'll also think of additional questions to ask and rabbit trails to run down. That's all good. It's part of the process. Consider what I've offered here a *starter*. The end product should be a comprehensive profile of the position you're looking to fill and another profile of the person you're looking to fill it. These two profiles will help you to apply the advice that follows in the rest of this chapter.

Where and How to Look

Once you've got your position profiled out, it's time to start looking for the person who best aligns with what you sketched out. Starting with the list you made back in Chapter 8, take a look at your personal network. Check to see if any of your friends and associates line up with your vision. If they do, they'll be the first people you want to consider for the position. In my experience, once I've developed out my position and profile, my network has been the best place to find new team members.

Once you've exhausted your network, it's time to check with your partners and/or investors. Who in *their* network fits your persona? If you don't find anyone there, then it's time to cast a wider net. When it comes to finding a candidate for your position, the internet is full of ways to get the word out about your position and seek out qualified candidates. Here are just a few:

- Glassdoor
- ZipRecruiter
- Monster
- Facebook
- LinkedIn

Each of these tools affords you the opportunity to do a few basic things: advertise your position, solicit applicants, and research potential candidates. Obviously, platforms like Glassdoor and ZipRecruiter are designed for hiring and will give you a more robust set of tools to work with. Social Media sites like Facebook won't do that, but they will help you capture the interest of people who may not be looking for work. With LinkedIn's search tools, you can specifically target people inside or outside of your network and talk to them about the position.

As you think about finding someone for your new position, don't forget to look at freelancers. Thanks to platforms like Upwork and Fiverr, freelancing has become an important part of Amercians' work life. According to Deloitte's "2019 Global Human Capital Trends Report," the number of self-employed workers in the U.S. will hit 42 million by 2020.[6] Remember Ron? We met through Upwork, and the value he brought to our business rivaled anything an in-house developer could've generated. Our business continues to use freelancers like Ron, and the results have been phenomenal.

Putting Your Players in the Field

While it's important to do and learn as much as you can in the beginning, there will come a time in your business when that's no longer feasible. Like I said in the previous chapter, you'll need to be able to hire and *trust* people to handle elements of the business that you don't entirely understand—at least, not at the level of technical detail. The beauty here is that you can hire smart, talented people to shore you up in the places you

---

[6] https://www2.deloitte.com/us/en/insights/focus/human-capital-trends.html

consider yourself dumb and talentless. That's not laziness; it's leadership.

As you bring new people onto the team, I can't stress the importance of building lanes. The last thing you want is your uber-talented team members drifting into one another's lane and wrecking the entire operation. For every position you design, then, make sure you're crystal clear about what that person is expected to do and where those expectations end. Once you've built the lane and set your team member free to drive, get out of the way and let them do what you've hired them to do. In other words, *you* need to stay in *your* lane. It's when leaders try to micromanage their team members that they create traffic and bring their organization to a snarling halt.

What to Say in the Locker Room

One of the most important things a coach does for his or her team is keep them inspired. When you've only got 5 players, that's not too complicated. But when you find yourself trying to inspire 40+ team members, things get a bit more complex. At that point, your people are no longer part of the building; they're part of the system. You can't inspire people one-on-one the same way a high school basketball coach would. Instead, you need to get intentional and systematic. In other words, you need to put systems in place that allow you to shape the motivational structure of your company.

One way to do that is to get intentional about what psychological drivers you want your people to bring with them onto the team. As you do your early profile work , consider the sorts of motivators you want to see in that new hire. Personally, I put a premium on people who devote themselves to self-improvement. I don't care how talented you are; if you think there's nothing left for you to learn or there's no room left for you to grow, then you won't be a good fit on my team. Another key motivator to consider is money. Should the person you're looking to hire be driven by his or her desire to make a pile of cash? Maybe. If you're hiring a salesperson to work on commission, then that might be an important motivator to look for. If you're hiring someone to do creative work, however, then you'll probably want more *intrinsic* motivators like a desire for excellence and a passion for aesthetics.

Speaking of money, money is *not* the best way to engage and inspire your employees. Of course, you need to pay your people a competitive wage. But once you've taken care of people's needs by compensating them fairly, the best things you can do to inspire them are more personal than they are transactional. *Acknowledging* team members' contributions, showing genuine *appreciation*, and *affirming* their important to the company may sound squishy, but putting those three simple words (acknowledge, appreciate, affirm) into practice will do infinitely more to engage your team members than a $250 check at Christmas. The basic point is this: Treat people the way you'd want to be treated. Celebrate in them what you'd like others to celebrate in you. See the best in them, and encourage them to live into the best version of themselves. Do that, and you'll inspire your team members to show up everyday and do their best work for you.

As a leader, you can't just inspire *individuals*. You need to inspire the team as a whole. At UTP, I try to do that by openly sharing the trials we've experienced through the years. I regularly tell the stories I've told throughout this book as a way of sharing our history and binding us together around a common narrative. As I do, I challenge our team members to read the books that have shaped me as a leader. Whenever I come across new resources that stretch me in a positive direction, I share those as well. I do my best to live my commitment to personal improvement out in public. When people see that, they want to join me in improving themselves. When you challenge people to grow and they start to see the fruit of their effort, you create the kind of personal and professional momentum that drives entire companies forward toward success.

Conclusion

I'm not Chuck Daly and, as proud as I am of UTP, we still have a lot to learn before we can run the court like Johnson, Byrd, and company did back in 1992. But that's the point. The businesses who think they've "arrived" stagnate and fall. The companies that thrive are those who continually innovate and ask the hard question: how can we be better? As you build your team, resist the notion a few talented players will automatically carry you to dominance. That's just not how this works.

Start off slow and small. Wait to hire as long as you can. When it's time, think methodically about who you want to hire and then be ruthless about finding a candidate who fits the profile. Build them a lane and then let them drive. Encourage these players along the way, drawing on the motivators that best move *them* forward. As you do, rally everyone together as often as you can. In all, dedicate yourself to relentless growth. Do that, and you'll be well on your way to building your very own dream team.

The Best Things
in Life Are Free

"THE BEST THINGS IN LIFE ARE FREE. AND
IT IS IMPORTANT NEVER TO LOSE SIGHT OF
THAT. SO LOOK AROUND YOU. WHEREVER
YOU SEE FRIENDSHIP, LOYALTY, LAUGHTER,
AND LOVE...THERE IS YOUR TREASURE.

NEALE DONALD WALSCH

CHAPTER 13

On TV and in the pages of Fast Company, the entrepreneur's life looks like one big fantasy. It's romantic and exciting—full of exotic cars, expensive vacations, and oversized houses. But if I've tried to communicate anything in writing this book, it's this: real entrepreneurship is more gritty and less glamorous than the media makes it out to be. My story isn't the exception here; it's the *rule*. If you decide to go into business for yourself, you're going to have trouble. That's just the way it is.

So, why do it? Why not take a safe job with a paycheck, work your way up, pay your dues, and someday enjoy a comfortable lifestyle near the top half of the corporate ladder? Those are good questions, and I'm not here to answer them for you. In fact, the corporate life might just be the best move *for you.* If you've read this far, though, then my guess is you're looking for something more than all that. I know I was (and still am). While that "something more" involves more than words can really say, there's one that sums it up better than any other: freedom. Let me explain.

The Yearning to be Free

Wake up at 6 AM on a Monday. Take a shower. Put on a shirt and tie. Eat breakfast. Get in the car. Show up at the office at 8 AM. Sit in front of a computer until noon. Eat lunch. Go back to your computer and grind away until 2 PM. Run to and from meetings until 5 PM. Get in your car. Sit in traffic for an hour. Eat dinner at 6:30 PM. See what's on Netflix at 7 PM. Tool around on Facebook at 9 PM. Pass out at 10 PM. Monday's a wrap. Rinse and repeat until the weekend.

I don't know about you, but that last paragraph just about drove me insane. The idea of repeating the exact same routine day-in, day-out strikes me as something a robot would do—not a human being. That's the problem with most of corporate life today; it's dehumanizing. It either reduces people down to productivity machines or, worse, it treats them like slaves. Nobody's holding you against your will, but your mortgage, car payment, and Junior's future college tuition have you chained to your desk. On this life plan, your only shot at freedom comes when you turn 67—at least, if you're fortunate enough to have had a little extra scratch to save for retirement.

Entrepreneurship sets you free from that daily grind. That's not to say that being an entrepreneur is the lazy man's way out. Again, this whole book has been written to show you how much *harder* it is to start your own thing. But, as hard as it may be, the freedom to engage your full humanity in your work, design your own schedule, and pour your sweat into something that advances *your* dreams—not somebody else's—is worth far more than the "stability" that comes with that 6x8 prison cell my corporate friends lock themselves into everyday between the hours of 8 and 5.

Free to Be Free

Freedom isn't just about the things we *don't* have to do (put on a tie, sit in traffic, sit in a cubicle, etc.). We often think of freedom as a negative concept: to be free is to be free from something like an overbearing boss or a mind-numbing commute. That's all true, but it's only half the story. When we're set free from the things that hold us back, we're set free to pursue the things we truly desire. If I'm free from the demands of an overbearing boss, for example, that means I'm free to become an inspiring leader to others. In that sense, freedom doesn't just break us away from something; it propels us toward something else.

Let's say you go out to fly a kite. Now, let's say you get the idea to set the kite free by cutting its string. What would happen? That kite would use its freedom to plummet straight to the ground! Why? Because a kite is essentially a sail. Without the string to keep it oriented, the chaotic winds will toss it in every direction *other* than the one it's supposed to go. Human beings are much the same. Like the kite, we're "constrained" by the deeply-held values that guide our thoughts and actions. While I'm technically "free" to abandon my family, the very idea hits me more as failure than freedom. Why? Because it rubs against the values of love and loyalty—*my* kite strings—that I've worked down deep into my bones. In that sense, I *can't* go. The freedom that says I can *leave* is the freedom that constrains me to *love*, not because I *have* to but because I *want* to.

Learning to use our freedom well isn't at all unique to entrepreneurs. What is unique, though, is our chance to do it *at work*, and to freely orient that work within our overall sense of purpose in life (more on that below). When you're an entrepreneur, you don't *have* to be a nameless worker bee, but you *get* to work your tail off. You don't *have* to be a slave to your desk, but you *get* to sit down and make things happen. You don't have to pretend like the customer's always right (he's not), but you *get* to find creative ways to take care of his needs.

When you spend 8-9 hours a day working away to realize a vision you don't believe in, you'll struggle to feel like anything more than a modern-day slave. But when you live in that space where all your hard work is fueled by *your* desire to achieve *your* dreams, you'll feel more free than you ever have in your entire life. Entrepreneurial freedom breaks us free from our chains. More importantly, though, it gives us the freedom to live and work for something more than a paycheck and a 401k.

The Freedom to Live on Purpose

What are we living and working for? That question has gotten a lot of play lately. Thanks to the growing number of millennials in the workforce, we are in the midst of what I call the Purpose Revolution. People want to know what they're supposed to do with their lives. More than ever, we're all wondering who we are and why we're on this planet. At work, in particular, we're eager to discover how our jobs help or hurt our pursuit of this grander purpose. If we're going to chain ourselves to a desk, we at least want to know that the work we're doing accomplishes some greater good in the world.

While wiser and more progressive companies have been willing to encourage their employees in this search for meaning and purpose, too much of corporate America is designed to pare down our individuality and slot us into the corporate machine. In the machine, our core purpose is to shut up and get the job done. When the proverbial whistle blows and we all head home, we're just too tired to think big thoughts about our life's purpose and whether our jobs move us closer to or further away from that ideal. So, we drop back into the routine. Eventually, we tamp down those thoughts and go back to merely existing—day to day, paycheck to paycheck, vacation to vacation.

When you're an entrepreneur, you get to drop out of the purposeless rat race and start living for something. In fact, if you're going to succeed in business, you pretty much have to live with a sense of unrelenting purpose. That deep purpose—what real estate guru Gary Keller calls the "Big Why"—is the only thing that can power you through the inevitable slog of entrepreneurship. Without a keen sense of who you are, what you're trying to accomplish, and why it matters, you'll never find the grit you need to power your way forward in the face of adversity. Without a driving sense of purpose, you'll fold as soon as a partner bails or a lawsuit lands in your mailbox.

But purpose isn't only about motivation. It's also about fulfillment. 40 years from now, when you look back over the course of your career, what do you want to see? If you've found the reason you were placed on this earth, then you'll want to be able to look at the work you've done and say that it's honestly helped you fulfill that purpose. For some, a corporate 9-5 will genuinely provide that sense of fulfillment. For most, it won't. For entrepreneurs—at least, for *this* entrepreneur—building a business and empowering others to pursue their own purpose through it will be more than enough for me to look back and confidently say, "That's what I was supposed to do with my life."

Creating Freedom for Others

In some of the more romantic pictures of entrepreneurship, you get the vision of a solo superstar who rose to the top on his or her own. In reality, though, nobody gets anywhere without the help of others. Every Steve Jobs has his Steve Wozniak. Every Lennon has his McCartney. Every Warren Buffett has his Charlie Munger. Being free to work for yourself doesn't mean you have to work *by* yourself.

When we only think about its negative side, we misread freedom as an opportunity to blow off everybody else and go our own way. While it's true that entrepreneurial freedom means nobody gets to be our master, nothing about that means we can't *choose* to use our freedom to serve others. It's in that voluntary service (notice, I didn't say voluntary slavery) that entrepreneurial freedom comes into full bloom.

One of the ways I get to serve the people who work for me is by extending to them the same freedom I've come to enjoy. Yes, I'm the boss, so they can't be *completely* autonomous. But there's plenty of space between making the rules and playing by them. Remember what I said in Chapter 11 about hiring talented people, setting expectations, and then staying out of their lane? That's precisely what I mean by extending freedom. Entrepreneurs get to hire fantastic people, point them in a direction, and then let them loose to engage their full humanity and creativity for the good of the company.

Done right, the lane you draw for your employees can be a wonderful space for exploration and creativity. In that place, they can discover their own passion and purpose. They can hone their skills and develop new ones. They identify problems and discover solutions that you never would've imagined. To bring back the kite metaphor, they're "tied down" to your organization, but you're letting the spool roll and cheering like crazy as you watch that sucker soar up into the clouds.

Everybody wins in that scenario. My team members get to grow into the best version of themselves. My company gets to reap the benefits of their increased value. Our workplace gets infused with energy. People genuinely fall in love with their work and look forward to coming into the office everyday. Customers catch wind of that and buy more of our products. Investors see what we're doing and decide they want in on the action. Outsiders look at our operation and say they want to be a part of it. Why? All because of the freedom I've been given to help others own their freedom and thrive in it.

Conclusion

Life as an entrepreneur has given me so much more than words could ever say. But if I had to pick a word, *freedom* gets closer than any other to summing up *why* it's all been worth it. Entrepreneurship is hard. Adversity will come, you'll fall flat on your face, and you won't always *feel* free—especially when you're putting in 14-hour days. But there will come a time when the dust settles and you look back over what you've accomplished. There, you'll discover what you've been working for all along—your purpose. And when you look at all the people you've served along the way, you'll realize that the true freedom you enjoy in that place is worth infinitely more than whatever you might've found in corporate America.

CHAPTER 14

You Get
What You Give

**YOU CAN HAVE EVERYTHING IN
LIFE YOU WANT IF YOU JUST HELP
ENOUGH OTHER PEOPLE GET WHAT
THEY WANT.**

ZIG ZIGLAR

One of the most important rules I've learned in life is this: *you get what you give.* You don't have to believe in Karma to recognize that whatever you put out into the world will inevitably come back to you. Love others, and they'll love you back. Help people, and they'll help you. In business, this dynamic plays out in lots of different ways. When you *give* money to sponsor an event, for example, you *get* the benefit of having your brand associated with a worthy cause. When you *give* merchandise to help stock a silent auction, you *get* the benefit of brand recognition along with the chance to put your product in more people's hands. Corporate giving isn't just the right thing to do; it's good business. The more you give, the more you get in terms of public recognition and good will. You can call this strategic giving, and it's a crucial part of any business with long-term hopes of success.

As important as strategic giving is, though, it isn't the whole ballgame. In this chapter, I'm going to help you develop a habit of giving. Before I do, though, I want to offer a word of warning. It's entirely possible that you could dial into the *getting* part of this chapter so much so that you turn the *giving* into a mere means to an end. That'd be a mistake. True giving has to come from the heart. If it doesn't, your giving will become a form of manipulation. That may work for a little while, but people know when they're being handled. They also know when you're only giving because you want something. Worse, that kind of *faux* giving is impossible to sustain. It's only when your giving flows naturally from a deep sense of gratitude for your success and concern for others that you'll be able to cultivate a habit of genuine, selfless giving that endures.

Learning to Serve

Most of the time, service doesn't come natural to us. In our day, pretty much everything is optimized to give us exactly what we want exactly when we want it. In the suburbs, I'm only 10 minutes away from virtually everything I could ever possibly need. On the rare occasion when I'd have to pierce that 10-minute bubble, I could always choose to stay home and have Amazon deliver whatever I'm looking for—sometimes within the next hour! From online shopping to food delivery to neighborhood healthcare, everything in my suburban life is set up to to one thing: serve me. Odds are, you can relate.

Don't get me wrong; I love the convenience of modern life, and I've got nothing against the capitalism that drives it. Still, one of the negative aspects of a culture where everything is at our fingertips is the mistaken idea that everything is always about me. When the customer's experience is at the center of every company's game plan—as it absolutely must be in today's environment—all our retail experiences train us to expect everyone and everything to serve us. Doubt that? Think about the last time you had to wait more than 5 minutes for a coffee. There's no judgment here; you and I breathe the same all-about-me air. And it's causing us to habitually move throughout our lives with one focus: what can I *get* here?

If we're going to learn to *give* in a world that's training us to *get*, we've got to be deliberate and intentional. Big gestures won't do it, nor will vague commitments to "being more generous" or "doing some community service." Instead, you've got to start small with concrete actions you can sustain over the long haul. What does that look like? Begin with your home. What's one simple thing you can do to serve your partner, spouse, roommate, or neighbor today? Make it as practical as you can: do the laundry, wash the car, pick up a cup of coffee, etc. Tomorrow, choose something else. Then, take it to the office or school, finding simple ways to serve the people you spend each day with. Make a commitment to do one concrete act of service every day for the next month. When the month is over, ramp up your efforts by going out of your way to serve people you normally don't come into contact with. Find a local food pantry to work in or a school to volunteer at. Give up an hour of your time every week serving people who you'll probably never meet again and who aren't in a position to return the favor.

What's the point of all this? Like diet or exercise, service is a habit. Developing new habits takes intentionality and perseverance. If you stick with the habit, though, the habit will stick with you. You'll gradually become a person who defaults to service in both small and big ways. You'll become the man or woman who's always looking out for others and leaning in to help. You won't be thinking about opportunities to serve; you'll just be the kind of person who intuitively sees them and dives in. It's only when you become that kind of person that you'll be able to weave giving into the core of your company and keep it there for as long you're in business.

You're in the Service Business

No matter what industry you're in, you're in the service business. Whether you're dealing with external clients or internal customers (i.e., your employees, partners, and investors), your job as a leader is to take care of people. On the consumer side, that's just obvious. Satisfied external customers will repeat business and tell their friends to check you out. Well-served internal customers will thrive in the roles you've carved out for them and help move the company forward. Good leaders are servants; they embrace their authority as a means for equipping and empowering others—not for puffing themselves up.

So far, we've looked at the kind of service that permeates the interior of a business. What about the service that extends outside the company's walls? There are plenty of ways in which your business can serve others. The most obvious way is through cold, hard cash donations. There's nothing wrong with that. Non-profit organizations need money to keep the lights on and do their work.

Who should you give to? While there's a lot of good being done by national and global organizations, I want to put a strong plug in for *local* giving. All business is local—even online business—in the sense that none of us work in a vacuum. Wherever you are in the world, you're embedded in one or more communities. Giving money to organizations that are poised to serve those communities is a great way to not just improve your personal quality of life but to signal to your neighbors that your business recognizes its place in the community and wants to play a part in its health. Local giving is good citizenship; it'll help your business lay down roots that can sustain it for years to come.

When it comes to giving, the best kinds often sync up with our work in meaningful ways. For example, my company runs through a ton of paper with all the posters we print out. In consideration of all those dead trees, we've committed to planting new ones in their place. It may seem insignificant, but this move is highly relevant to our business and it signals our respect for and commitment to our world. Another example would be our donated apparel. Whenever we misprint and misrun a batch of apparel, we donate it to people in need instead of recycling or throwing it away. Grocery stores like Whole Foods and restaurants like Panera do this all the time when they donate unsold food to local homeless shelters at the end of each day.

The opportunities here are virtually endless. And there's plenty of space for you to be creative. What's your business's unique value proposition? What do you bring to the world that sets you apart? Is there a need in your community that resonates with your core offering? Are you in a position to offer your product or service—at a lower scale, of course— for free? Take your time to think through the answers to those questions. There, you'll find a treasure trove of opportunities to meaningfully serve your community.

Another way to brainstorm relevant ways to serve is by thinking carefully about your organizational values and how they might benefit the community. What do you and your company value the most? Where do you see those values lacking in your community? How can your business act to promote them? A simple example here would be the NFL's Play 60 program. As a professional sports league, the NFL values health and physical fitness. So, they've developed a program where professional athletes give up their time to encourage kids to get out and exercise. It's a simple, yet powerful way to promote values the league holds dear, and it matches up perfectly with the NFL's brand.

Building A Company that Serves

I can't say that giving has always been on my entrepreneurial radar. For the first few years of my business, I was too busy trying to do my own thing to think all that much about anyone outside my circle. That all changed, though, when I read Blake Mycoskie's *Start Something That Matters*. If the name doesn't sound familiar to you, Mycoskie is the founder of TOMS shoes. He started the company back in 2006 with the simple idea of giving away a pair of shoes for every pair he sold. 13 years later, TOMS has given away millions of shoes to needy people all over the world. As I read his book, I was struck by the simplicity of his vision and his relentless pursuit to do work that matters. From him, I learned that giving is good for business, the world, and your soul. He inspired me to get intentional about how we would use UTP as a force for good.

TOMS was able to do good *and* turn a healthy profit, all because Mycoskie wove giving into its DNA from the start. Whether your company shares that early commitment or not, it's never too late to start. Part of your battle in creating a culture of giving, though, will be similar to what you'd experience in cultivating your own habit of service. People aren't accustomed to focusing on others. That said, introduce giving into your company the same way you would your own life. Begin with small, concrete tasks. Encourage your team members to serve one another in simple, everyday ways. Then, layer in more intentional opportunities to serve: a community clean-up day, regular mentoring at a local school, etc. Give them the time and space to serve in these ways. Consider it an investment in culture. When you give your team members the freedom to serve others, what you'll get in return are better people who habitually look out for one another at work.

When it comes to giving and service, sustainability is the name of the game. One of the worst things you could do to a community or a volunteer organization is show up, let them begin to depend on you, and then flake out over time. As a leader, then, it'll be on you to weave giving into your company's culture in a way that you can keep up with. If it's encouraging your team members to volunteer x number of hours per week, you need to commit to protecting that time no matter what else is going on in the business. If it's money, then you need to be upfront with that organization about what they can expect from you and when. Be generous, but don't give more than you can sustain in terms of time or money. A little bit, faithfully given over the long haul, will be far more helpful than a few unpredictable gifts.

Conclusion

Giving back to your community and your world is one of the most important things you can do as an entrepreneur. We've been given this incredible opportunity to build things that matter; it'd be a shame if we squandered it. At the end of the day, that's the conviction that drove me to write this book. This project is a form of giving for me—a sharing of the knowledge I've gleaned from my 15 years as an entrepreneur. I want you to learn from my experience so that you can go out and build something that matters to you and the world around you. What do I stand to gain from all this? Not much. After all, you've already bought the book! But that doesn't matter, because genuine giving is its own reward. And when you get to the place where you can sincerely rest in the joy of giving for its own sake, you'll be amazed at what you get in return.

Glitter Tattoos, Entrepreneurial Vision, and a World Full of Opportunity

CHAPTER 15

> "YOU ARE THE AVERAGE OF THE FIVE PEOPLE YOU SPEND THE MOST TIME WITH.
>
> JIM ROHN

W hen my daughter, Addison, was 8 years old, a friend of mine gave her a crisp $20 bill to do with as she pleased. So, she hopped on Amazon and bought herself a glitter tattoo kit. For a while, that thing just sat in her room and collected dust. But, when tournament season kicked into full swing a few months later, she trotted the kit out and declared that she'd be selling tattoos at my next event. Sure enough, it only took her a few days to sell all 150 of those tattoos for a buck a piece. Not a bad margin for anybody—let alone an 8-year-old. But the story doesn't end there. Instead of laughing her way to the bank, my little girl dragged me down to Hobby Lobby so that she could spend her profit on a brand new airbrush set. Why? Addison figured she could sell more tattoos if she used an airbrush. Of course, she'd never used an airbrush before, so she had to spend a few late nights perfecting her craft before she could set up shop again. When she did, though, her airbrushed tattoos were a huge success. All told, she ended up taking my friend's initial $20 investment and turning into a couple hundred dollars.

I love that story, and I don't think it ever would've happened had I not decided to become an entrepreneur. My career has allowed me to weave together life and business, home and work. I've seen that go really poorly for some, but it's allowed me to integrate what I've learned in the business world with what I teach my kids about life. Make no mistake; the golden nugget of the story I told you above wasn't "here's how to build a business on a shoe-string budget." While it surely includes that, the deeper lesson my daughter learned and embodied was one of self-improvement, perseverance, and value. She saw the chance to provide a valuable service, so she jumped on it. Then, she used her initial success to increase her skills and bump up her value. Nobody told her to do that; it was just "in" her. Why? Because, for her entire life, she's watched me do the same thing in my business and listened when I told her how it all worked.

Throughout this book, I've leaned hard on the idea that *you become what you're around.* Surround yourself with people who've succeeded in life, and some of their success will rub off on you. Join a pity party with those who haven't, and you'll never challenge yourself to do better. In my family, I've watched this dynamic play out as my kids become little entrepreneurs just like their dad. They've watched me live the stories I've written down in this book. On the baseball field, around the dinner table, and sitting in my home office, our children have picked up on the many lessons I've had to learn over the past 14 years of blood, sweat, and tears. It's crazy, but I see it in the way they think about the world and their place in it. Exhibit A: Addison's tattoo business.

In this chapter, I'll tell you a bit more about my kids, specifically Addison—the oldest and most entrepreneurial in the bunch. This isn't about bragging on my children, though I do love to do that. It's about making a point: you become what you're around. The fact that my kids have learned to see the world through entrepreneurial eyes and think about it as a place of limitless opportunity tells me something about what they've seen in me. More important for you as a reader, it speaks volumes about the value of what I've shared so far in this book.

Use What You've Got

The first time I glimpsed the entrepreneurial spark in Addison was when she was 4 years old. We were at a hockey game and she wanted money to play at the arcade, but my wife and I weren't ready to cough up the cash. So, what'd she do? Instead of pouting or throwing a fit, she grabbed the bag of snacks and toys we had brought for her, laid them all out on a table, and started shouting at the top of her lungs, "Snacks for $1!" Within a few minutes, she sold the whole bag and headed off to the arcade with $10 in her hand. I'm pretty sure the stuff in that bag cost me more than $10. That didn't matter to her, though. That ten bucks was pure margin.

In our family life and in my business, we've always tried to be thrifty. We're not cheap, by any means, but we know how important it is to make the most of your resources. At home, our kids have never seen us try to live above our means. Instead, we've chosen to live small and make the most of everything. At work, I'm constantly looking for ways to minimize costs and maximize efficiency. That's how we've been able to create a streamlined process that scales. Whatever the venue, my wife and I have focused on utilizing our resources to the absolute best of our ability. Our kids have seen that, and they've learned not to take things for granted. While other kids would sit and complain about not having what they want, my kids have learned to appreciate what they've got.

Thriftiness is a valuable lesson for anyone to learn—not just 4-year-olds. As an entrepreneur, you'll have plenty of opportunities to make a lot out of a little. It goes with the territory. In those times when you need to tighten your bootstraps and dig deep, you probably won't have the luxury of asking your parents to bail you out. When you find yourself in that place, act like my 4-year-old. Grab your bag of tricks, lay them all out, and start hollering at the top of your lungs until you get yourself where you need to go.

Seize the Opportunity

I'll never forget the day Addison's mom called to complain about the mess Addison had just made in the kitchen. While mom was upstairs getting ready for a picnic with friends, what did Addison do? She got into the fridge and pantry, grabbed out all the fixin's for sandwiches. Why? Apparently, she was planning to make the sandwiches and tote them along to the park to sell to all her mom's friends. There she went again, grabbing whatever resources she could find in order to turn a profit.

The thing I love most about this story isn't my daughter's resourcefulness. Instead, it's her eye for an opportunity. She knew she was going to a picnic. She also knew that sandwiches are a great thing to have at a picnic and there'd be people there with money to burn. As far as she could see, there was a sandwich-shaped hole in the picnic market and she had the goods to fill it. All that was left was for her to get to work.

Kids are narcissists by design. They aren't usually primed to see the world in terms of opportunities to provide value. They tend to ask "what can you do for me" rather than "what can I do for you." The most successful people in life, though, are those who learn to master the second question. When you understand others' needs, you put yourself in a position to fulfill them. That, folks, is the essence of business. From smartphones to microwave ovens, the world's greatest products have focused on looking into the market and providing solutions to the real problems customers face every day. In whipping up those sandwiches, Addison demonstrated a keen insight into what *other* people want and how she might give it to them—even if she made a mess in the process.

Give the People What They Want

This past summer, Addison got the idea for something like a pop-up bakery. So, she convinced her Grandma Patty to front the cash for supplies. Her plan was simple: bake the cookies, sell the cookies. Unfortunately, the second prong in that plan failed and she only ended up making a dollar. When I asked her what happened, she was as blunt as she was clear about what had gone wrong. Instead of throwing up her hands and blaming the market for not responding to her offering, she plainly said: "It was 100 degrees outside; I should've sold snow cones." Smart girl.

You can complain all you want when things don't go your way, but it takes courage and insight to acknowledge what *you* did wrong. Kids *and* adults often struggle to own their mistakes. As a result, they miss out on some of life's most valuable lessons. Earlier in the book, I emphasized the value of adversity for your personal growth. I stand by that. I wouldn't be who I am today if it weren't for the hard lessons I've learned along the way. Mistakes and failures are our greatest teachers, but only if you're willing to listen to what they have to say. When you shift the blame, you shut your ears and doom yourself to a lifetime of repeated mistakes.

Conclusion

I could go on for days about Addison and her many forays in the entrepreneurial world. My friends, neighbors, and team members have all found themselves on the receiving end of one of her many "sales pitches." I love that about my daughter, and I'm so grateful for having had the opportunity to teach her how to use her ingenuity to bring value to other people's lives. But like I said at the beginning of this chapter, the point of these stories wasn't to brag on my kids. Instead, I wanted you to see that we truly do become what we're around. The lessons I've shared in this book are the same insights that have formed my children, and the eyes through which they see the world will forever be "corrected" by the entrepreneurial lens they picked up from their father.

Most adults—let alone kids—will never learn to look for opportunity the way Addison has. That's a shame, because the kinds of opportunities that lead to success are all around us. They don't belong to an elite group of natural-born entrepreneurs; they belong to *everybody*. All you need is a set of eyes that have been formed through constant practice to look carefully at the world. Based on what you see, you need to learn how to ask good questions. What do I have to offer the world? Who in the world would benefit from the value I have to bring? What are people looking for, how does that relate to what they truly need, and how can I step in to provide meaningful solutions?

These questions, along with the quest to find your way into the vast marketplace that is the world, point to both the privilege and the pain of entrepreneurship. Interacting with the world in this way is hard; it takes fearlessness and willingness to live outside the status quo. The more you'll engage your entrepreneurial vision, though, the more naturally you'll see opportunity. More importantly, the easier it'll be for you to step in and seize your moment when it presents itself. Whether that moment is a kids' softball tournament, an afternoon picnic, or a market crying out for disruption, you'll know it when you see it. And, just like my daughter, you'll be so excited that *nothing* will stop you from piecing together the resources you need to make your vision a reality.

Something More Useful Than a Conclusion

> **" I KNEW THAT IF I FAILED I WOULDN'T REGRET THAT, BUT I KNEW THE ONE THING I MIGHT REGRET IS NOT TRYING.**
>
> JEFF BEZOS, FOUNDER AND CEO OF AMAZON

Throughout this book, I've tried to toe the line between interesting stories and practical advice. As much as I love to tell my story, what matters most to me is that you would learn something from my experience. That's why I've broken up the narrative to provide simple advice for navigating the challenges I faced along the way. In this final chapter, I want to bring things to a close on that same practical note by sharing some of the most valuable resources I've discovered over the years. Paired with the advice I shared in chapter 6, these books, apps, and platforms will help you take care of the stuff that truly matters so that you can get your business off the ground as quickly as possible.

5 of The Most Important Books I've Read

Books have been some of my greatest teachers in life. The books, in particular, have shaped my outlook on business more than any other:

1. **Napoleon Hill, *Think and Grow Rich*** — This is a classic and a must-read for anyone who's serious about getting into business. In it, Hill teaches his readers how to engage their subconscious mind to master their emotions and move confidently towards *any* goal—not just making a ton of money.

2. **Jim Collins, *Good to Great*** — Another classic, this book dissects how companies move from good to great by focusing on disciplined people, disciplined thought, and disciplined action. Some of the concepts in this book (Level 5 Leadership, the Bus, the Hedgehog Concept) have deeply influenced me.

3. **David Allen, *Getting Things Done*** — This book is the gold standard in productivity and time management. The core focus for Allen is encouraging stress-free productivity. How? By managing the open loops in our lives, mastering our workflow, and fighting off the feeling of 'overwhelm.'

4. **Stephen R. Covey, *The 7 Habits of Highly Effective People*** — This book taught me that if we change our perception, we change our world. To reliably change our perceptions, though, we need to put on habits that will change us from the inside out. True self-improvement is about character—not strategy.

5. **Eric Schmidt & Jonathan Rosenberg, *How Google Works*** — In a world dominated by Google, this book will help you understand how businesses are built today. In it, the authors show how technology has altered the power dynamic between companies and customers. The only way to win in the new dynamic is to attract "smart creatives" and unleash their full power.

10 Essential Apps for Business

Technology has woven itself into the fabric of our lives and businesses. You *can't* run a business today without a little help from the following apps (or their equivalents):

1. **Slack** – Slack is a robust messaging tool that will help you and your team keep track of your communication much better than email ever could. We swear by it.
2. **Zoho** – Zoho is a one-stop shop for customer relationship management (CRM), email, data, storage, and expense reports. This is a crucial tool for our company.
3. **HubSpot** — HubSpot is another CRM, focused more heavily on sales and marketing. They've got a great free option for new businesses.
4. **OneNote** — OneNote is a great centralized note-taking program. You can clip items from pretty much anywhere and hold on to them for later use.
5. **Wunderlist** — Wunderlist is a simple task manager. There are tons of programs that do this, but most of them are much more complicated than they need to be.
6. **Zoom** — Zoom is a video conferencing tool like Skype. Both are good, but I've found Zoom to be more comprehensive and useful for our company.
7. **Team Viewer** — If you've got remote employees, you need a way to share screens and/or take control of their computer. Team Viewer helps us do just that.
8. **Zendesk** — Zendesk is pretty much a customer service department in a box. The program's got all the tools you need to take excellent care of your customers.
9. **Clockit** — Clockit makes time-tracking and reporting easy—especially

when you've got a distributed workforce like we have at UTP.

10. **Google Drive** — Along with Google's Docs, Sheets, and Slides apps, Drive makes collaborating and safeguarding important documents brain-dead simple.

3 Tools for Building a Starter Website

Building a website is easier than it's ever been. You'll eventually want to pay for a custom site. For now, though, these tools are exactly what you need to get started:

1. **Squarespace** — Squarespace is probably the most popular website-building platform right now. Of the 3 tools listed here, Squarespace offers the most flexibility in terms of visual design. It's not quite as easy to use as the others.

2. **Wix** — Wix isn't as flexible as Squarespace, but it's a great all-around website builder. It's got strong customer support and great all-around value.

3. **Weebly** — Weebly's great for small businesses. It's also got flexible pricing for smaller businesses. Be careful, though; it can get pricey as your site grows.

2 Ways to Get Paid

When I first started, I didn't even know how to take a credit card. Today, getting paid is as easy as plugging in your phone. Here are two of the best tools available:

1. **Square** — If you've ever seen someone stick a white square into their phone and run a credit card through it, then you've seen Square.

We swear by this company and use it to process credit card purchase at all of our sites.

2. **PayPal** — Customers can pay you with a credit card through PayPal, but only if they have an account. The platform is better for transferring money between vendors, contractors, and partners. They've also got a strong invoicing tool.

Make sure to google state sales tax laws. It's on you to collect and pay all applicable taxes and surcharges. Miss this and you'll end up paying through the nose in penalties.

A Parting Word

You've read my story, sifted through (I hope!) my practical advice, and checked out my list of essentials for getting started in and running a business. All that's left now is for you to come and join me on the entrepreneurial battlefield. The worst thing you could do, as far as I'm concerned, is close this book and put it back up on the shelf right next to that killer business idea you've been sitting on. If that's what you're getting ready to do, then I want to challenge you to fight against your fear. Take it from someone who's failed more times than he can remember: the only decision you're guaranteed to regret is the one you make to *not* pursue your entrepreneurial dream.

If you go into business for yourself, I promise you'll walk through plenty of adversity. It goes with the territory. But I can also promise that you'll learn more about yourself than you ever imagined. Most importantly, you'll find out that you have more to offer this world than any corporate suit or college professor will ever be willing to admit.

So what's it going to be? Are you ready to sell yourself into modern slavery? Or, do you want to take the road less traveled toward a life of freedom, purpose, and limitless opportunity? I hope this book has offered you a glimpse into what that journey could look like. The problems I started with (how to sneak a poster onto somebody's porch) look nothing like the problems I face today (how to coordinate with my teams in Mexico). 10 years from now, my problems will be far more complicated than anything I could imagine right now. That's a good thing. It means I haven't arrived yet. I've still got more road to travel. I've got more learning and growing to do.

Whoever you are—whether you've been in business for 20 days or 20 years—that will always be true. You will always have room to grow and learn. Your problems will never go away. If you're doing it right, they'll only grow more and more complex. So don't you dare let the fact that you haven't figured it all yet keep you from getting into the game. You're going to face adversity. It's going to hurt, but you're going to will yourself through it and grow in the process. You're going to have to solve "stupid" problems that cause your future self to look back and chuckle. You're going to take on projects you don't know how to manage, walk into sales meetings you don't know how to close, and put yourself into situations you don't know how to handle. Good. Lean into that uncertainty. Force yourself to figure things out as you go. Get serious about your dream and pursue it relentlessly. Do that, and you'll fail 100 times along the way but you'll never become a "failure." You know what you'll become instead? An entrepreneur.